PAINTING THE
TOWN RED

PAINTING THE TOWN RED

Noel Davidson

AMBASSADOR

BELFAST, NORTHERN IRELAND
GREENVILLE, USA

ISBN 1 84030 115 5

Ambassador Books
an imprint of
Ambassador Productions Ltd.
Providence House
Ardenlee Street,
Belfast,
BT6 8QJ
Northern Ireland
www.ambassador-productions.com

Emerald House
427 Wade Hampton Blvd.
Greenville
SC 29609, USA
www.emeraldhouse.com

CONTENTS

INTRODUCTION

On the first evening I went to visit him, Sammy was sitting with his Bible open.

"When the man from Ambassador rang me at the beginning of the week to ask me if I would agree to have my story written in a book, I spent some time praying to the Lord for guidance, and I believe He gave me this verse," he began to explain, after we had greeted one another. "The amazing thing is that I didn't even know it was in the Bible until a couple of days ago."

He then proceeded to read to me from Exodus chapter thirty-two, 'And the tables were the work of God, and the writing was the writing of God, graven upon the tables'.

Keeping his finger in the page Sammy closed his Bible gently and continued, "I feel we should pray that God will lead us in this project, Noel, that everything we say may be to His glory."

With that the prospective subject of my next biography bowed his head and started to thank God for saving the both of us and bringing us together under the circumstances, and to pray that my writing might be guided by God. When he had finished praying I followed, and so within fifteen minutes of meeting for the very first time we had shared the Scriptures and prayed together.

That could only be a promising beginning.

What Sammy didn't know, though, was that when 'the man from Ambassador' as he called him, had phoned me to discuss the possibility of writing this book, he had described to me a meeting he had attended in which Sammy had related his life story.

"It was," he said, "a real roller coaster of emotions. One minute the people were smiling and the next they were almost in tears."

What a combination! And what a challenge for an author!

To record the obviously emotive story of a man whose prime concern was that when recounted it should be recognised as having been guided by God.

Over the months following that initial encounter and as I began to research this story I realized why the congregation had been so touched by it that winter evening.

It has all the essential ingredients.

There is the faithful Sunday School teacher who warned an erring pupil, in a spirit of love and grace, 'Be sure your sin will find you out.' And those words never left him.

There is the painter who embarked upon his career by painting the walls and pavements of his hometown red, white and blue. He progressed from that to setting up his own painting and decorating business, and finished up, through the exercise of his skills as a craftsman, being introduced to a work which was destined to change the entire focus of his life, in a foreign country.

Then there is the love story. Sammy and his love for Libby. His big problem at one stage was that if he trusted in Jesus, he thought that Libby would leave him. That would be some choice to have to make.

I haven't mentioned the funeral yet either, or the boys from The Blue Star Flute Band, or the U.D.A. council meetings.

The main theme of this story, and it pervades every chapter, indeed every page, is how God in His love and mercy called one of the most notorious characters in a small country town to Himself, and turned his life around completely.

That transformation, which had been considered impossible by his friends and neighbours, soon became very evident to them when they observed that the life of Sammy Graham had taken off in a completely new direction. For he began to throw himself into the work of God with exactly the same one hundred per cent commitment he had once displayed when painting murals, designing uniforms or beating the Lambeg drum in his earlier day.

God has used that dedication to allow Sammy to see much done to help further the spread of the gospel, both in his home country and in Russia.

And the Russian connection is a saga in itself. There we are introduced to a whole range of fascinating characters like Vera and Valya, and Yula and Yana, to name but a few. Many of these faithful Christian people have had fantastic experiences in the course of their simple service for the Lord, themselves...

This book represents in truth, a roller coaster ride through the emotions.

Our prayer is that it may appear to you, not as the words of its subject, or of its author, but as a message from God.

For then it will lead you to faith in Christ if you do not already know Him, or to love Him and serve Him more diligently if you do.

Noel I. Davidson.
October 2001.

Chapter One

WAITING FOR THE NOD

"Aunt Annie, can I lift that money some day?" the eight year old enquired eagerly, his eyes dancing.

"No, Samuel, sorry you can't. The bigger boys and girls do that," came the firm reply.

But young Sammy Graham wasn't going to be put off that easily. Two weeks later he repeated his request.

"Aunt Annie, can I lift that money today?" he asked again, with as much enthusiasm as before.

"No, Samuel, son. I told you the last time. There are bigger people to do that!" The response was just as firm, and apparently just as final as it had been before, also.

No harm to 'the bigger people', Sammy thought, but that's a great job they have. All they have to do is go round with a basket and everybody throws money into it, for nothing. They don't have to work or anything. They just lift loads of money. And they must get keeping it, too, for who else would want it?

'Aunt Annie', as the children attending Ballynahinch Congregational Church Sunday School were encouraged to call

Annie Magowan, who was a local business woman and their Sunday School teacher, wouldn't need it. Sammy always thought she was beautifully dressed and he was sure she had a posh house somewhere, too. So she would definitely have no need of it. And all the other men and women who taught in the Sunday School seemed fairly well off as well, so they wouldn't need it either.

The only sensible thing would be to allow the people who collected it to keep it. That would be the only fair way!

And that was the first job that Sammy Graham really coveted.

He would just love to be a Sunday School collection collector.

So he would keep asking, and if he kept at it one day Aunt Annie might listen to him. Some day maybe all the 'bigger boys and girls' might catch the flu or something, and then he would get to fulfil his boyhood ambition.

Sammy loved Sunday School, and every one of the Sunday School teachers. They had all been so good to him since he had first begun to attend as a four year old. And Aunt Annie was no exception. She was very kind to the thirteen or fourteen eight and nine year olds in her class. She knew them all well and seemed so caring when she talked to them. Everybody mattered to her.

What really made Sammy think she was great, though, was the way she told them Bible stories. When Aunt Annie had finished telling about Abraham who nearly killed his son Isaac, or David who did kill Goliath with one shot of a stone from a sling, or Daniel with a crowd of lions roaring round him, Sammy thought he had just been there. He had paid a fleeting visit back a few thousand years. In fact he felt that he knew characters like Jacob and Joseph and Jonah just as well as some of the mates he played with down in Lisburn Street.

And at Christmas time Aunt Annie brought everybody presents all wrapped up in fancy paper, and talked with great joy, about 'good tidings of great joy', and the birth of Jesus. Then at Easter particularly, but dozens of other times, too, it seemed, that she told them about the death of Jesus on the cross. Sammy was almost sure he had seen tears in her eyes a time or two when she did this, and she always did it in a very sad and sorrowful voice.

Aunt Annie always explained to all the children in her class that it was for them as individuals, and for their sins, that Jesus had died.

Sammy struggled with that one. He could never really understand why a man who had never done anything wrong, as Aunt Annie had told them, would want to be nailed to a cross in a place called Jerusalem, thousands of miles away, for him, a very ordinary wee boy living in a very ordinary wee house in Ballynahinch, Northern Ireland.

Some day, perhaps, he would figure it out.

One thing he could figure out, though, was what he could do with that money in that plate or basket or whatever they called it, if he could get his hands on it!

So Sammy stuck at it.

"Aunt Annie, can I lift that money today?" was his question. Almost every Sunday.

"No, Samuel. I must have told you two dozen times already, it's the bigger boys and girls who do that," came the answer. Almost every Sunday.

Then one morning, all of a sudden, and out of the blue, Sammy's big day came.

Aunt Annie must either have been in a very good mood with him, or else in a very bad mood with everybody else, he reckoned, for when she had settled herself into her seat, she looked across to where he was sitting, second from the end of the opposite row, and asked, "Samuel, would you like to lift the collection today?"

"Praise the Lord!" Sammy half-said, half-shouted, without even half thinking about it. He knew that was what you said in this church when you were happy, for he had heard the adults at it. And he certainly was happy!

"Yes, Aunt Annie, I would love to!" he went on. "But what is it exactly that I have to do?"

"Oh Samuel, you have been on at me for months now to getting lifting the collection and you don't know what to do!" the friendly teacher laughed in mock surprise. "All you have to do is hold out the plate and the boys and girls will put their money into it!"

Sounded a real cinch to Sammy.

"O.K." he replied, smiling broadly.

And then something else dawned on him. There was another thing he needed to know.

"When do I do it, Aunt Annie?" he enquired. "I mean how will I know when to start?"

It was Aunt Annie's turn for the broad smile.

"Don't worry about that Samuel. When I come almost to the end of the lesson I will give you the nod," she assured him.

Sammy usually loved Aunt Annie's lessons, and remembered them for days.

But he didn't hear much of that one, or remember it for long.

In the snatches he caught of it he realized that it was something to do with a sower and seed. There seemed to be birds that ate some of the stuff, the sun that scorched some of it, and thorns that choked some of it. Sammy though, couldn't make much sense of it. For he wasn't concentrating on it.

He was waiting for the nod.

There were times when he thought that Aunt Annie had forgotten how to nod. Time was passing. Sunday school would soon be over. And still she hadn't nodded.

Then it came.

Just after she had finished a really serious bit about 'the good seed of the Gospel in the hearts of boys and girls', she looked across at Sammy, just as she had done when she came in at the first.

And gave him the nod!

Sammy was off his seat like a shot!

He remembered the instructions he had been given, too. 'Just hold out the plate and the boys and girls will put their money into it.'

It was fantastic!

As he walked around his own class all the boys and girls that he knew so well dropped in their big copper pennies. There were a good number of them in the soft green bottom of the plate, but it was nowhere near full. There must be a lot of money still to be collected in that room. And Sammy had a lot of room left on his plate.

So it was then that the newly appointed collection collector made his first mistake.

He went after it!

Totally oblivious to the fact that every class was supposed to be responsible for its own collection Sammy moved into the class beside his, and lifted the money there.

Then he moved into the class beside that again, and although he met with some puzzled glances from the 'bigger boys and girls' up there, they forked out their sweaty coins to the intrepid Sammy, as well. This must be some new way of lifting the collection, they concluded.

Everyone seemed rather bemused and the teachers looked across at one another with knowing and forgiving smiles, as the eight-year old Sammy went from class to class collecting everybody's money.

And Sammy could hardly believe it!

His plate was becoming heavier with every class.

Most of the coins were big copper pennies, but there were hexagonal 'three-penny bits', and a few shiny silver sixpences as well. It was mostly the older pupils who put them in. They must be richer, Sammy thought.

All those who watched in mild amusement as the busy collection lifter mover silently, but swiftly from class to class didn't realize that the enterprising little lad had a plan in his mind. But he had.

For he had carefully planned his collecting circuit so that his last stop would be beside the big grey doors at the back of the church hall.

Then when he was sure that he had relieved all the unwitting children of their weekly offering, he bolted. Out through the big grey doors he went, down the side of the church, and out on to the footpath, running as hard as his load would allow him!

Sammy Graham had never realized before, because he had never done it before, that he was a left-handed collection collector. That is, he had held the plate in his left hand, and that was where it had stayed. However he soon discovered that you couldn't run very hard down the street holding an open plate of money in one hand for it might spill. And he certainly didn't want to lose any of that money, not one brown penny. He had worked so hard to collect it, and in fact, on reflection, it was very kind of everybody to bring it for him. So he ended up running down the road past the Fire Station, holding his right hand over all the coins to keep them on the plate, and this, in turn, meant that he didn't have a hand for balance or thrust.

The end result was that Sammy was making for home as hard as he could go, to count his takings, writhing as he ran, like a duck in a hurry.

Suddenly he heard heavy breathing behind him.

Someone was running who wasn't used to running.

The firm fast footsteps were coming ever closer…

Then, in one startling, choking instant a gloved hand grabbed the back of his collar, and Sammy came to a half-strangled stop.

"I think… we had better… go back to the church… for a talk… Samuel," a voice said, coming in huge, breathless gasps.

And 'Samuel' knew the voice well.

He heard it every Sunday.

It was Aunt Annie.

Turning sheepishly, and without daring to look up, he wiggled as he walked back from whence he had come.

What was Aunt Annie making all the fuss about?

Did she really need some of that money after all?

Perhaps they could go fifty-fifty.

But by the way she was panting for breath, and by the way she was pounding back along the pavement, he didn't think he would suggest it.

Not yet anyway.

Chapter Two

GOD'S WORD AND
THE LORD'S MONEY

When the parading pair arrived back in the church building, Aunt Annie said, "Come into the vestry here, Samuel. I want to point out one or two wee verses to you from the Bible. There are just a few things I think you ought to know about what you have just done."

Sammy wondered what there was that he didn't know about what he had just done. He had merely lifted the collection and was on his way home with it, to count it, and then find a use for it, when she had caught up with him.

What else did he need to know?

Perhaps she **did** need it for something.

Maybe it was that.

"You sit down there anywhere while I put this money away safely somewhere until I get a moment to count it. Then I will fetch my Bible and return to you, Samuel," she said, rather stiffly, while waving an arm across at a choice of three chairs lined against the back wall.

As she was making for the door of the vestry with the collection, Aunt Annie turned around purposefully, and holding the plate out in front of her, like a crucial exhibit in a court case, declared, "You know Samuel, this is not your money, or my money, it is the Lord's money."

With that she bustled out, leaving the door ajar.

As Sammy sat there alone, in silent reflection, he had at least one matter cleared up in his mind. Aunt Annie was the Superintendent of the Sunday School and for a few minutes he had convinced himself that she **was** really going to be the sole benefactor of his labours. And she was going to be one unbelievably lucky woman for not only did she have a shop in the town, but she was going to get pocketing all that collection as well!

Now he knew, though, that even that was not the case.

It was the Lord's money.

That was one matter settled, and in no uncertain terms. But the solution to his first problem only left Sammy wrestling with a second, even more complex one.

The enterprising eight year-old began to try to come to grips with the question of why it was that the Lord who had made everything, who owned everything, and who controlled everything, according to Aunt Annie, would need the fifteen or sixteen bob on that plate. He was still all at sea with it when his teacher blustered back, bearing her Bible.

Then with a forgiving smile she sat down beside her slightly bewildered pupil.

Opening up the well-worn book on her knee, Aunt Annie prefaced her remarks by an all-embracive statement about the importance of whatever it was that she was preparing to read.

Samuel had felt encouraged by her wan smile, but soon he came to realize that he had only been fooled by it.

The stern, but still somehow strangely soothing tone had returned when she pronounced, "You must remember, Samuel, that these are not my words, these are not even the minister's words. What I am about to read to you Samuel, these are God's words."

In an attempt to emphasise her perceived total relevance of the words soon to be read, Aunt Annie then lifted the Bible from her knee, where it had slid over to the one side, and held it up about two feet from Samuel's face.

"Bear in mind, Samuel, that this is God's book," she continued, earnestly. "He told a whole lot of men what to write down and they did it, but always remember that these are God's words."

When satisfied that the moment of that particular message had sunk in upon the subdued Samuel, as she called him, Aunt Annie proceeded to read the Ten Commandments. And when she arrived at the one she had been aiming for she read it ever so soberly, "Thou shalt not steal."

And afraid that Samuel may have missed it, she repeated it.

"Thou shalt not steal.

Did you hear that, Samuel, 'Thou shalt not steal'?"

When the pupil on the spot had nodded assent, Aunt Annie carried on to explain, "You know that is not just a request from God. It is a command, Samuel. 'Thou shalt not steal'. And although you never thought of it at the time, what you were actually doing when you took that money out of the church was stealing."

Now Samuel had learnt something else.

He had never imagined that anybody would consider collecting and then claiming the Sunday school offering as stealing. But it seemed it was.

Having duly established by a series of simple words and sincere repetition, the gravity of 'breaking the commandments', Aunt Annie then flicked through the Bible a further few pages, and stopped.

She was all set up for stage two.

"Now listen to this, for again these are God's words, Samuel," she ordered her pupil, and not waiting for any possible response from him she pressed on to read aloud, 'Behold you have sinned against the Lord: and be sure your sin will find you out'.

There's the point. Stealing is sin, and sin against the Lord, but this verse tells you that you can't expect to get away with it either. It will catch up with you somewhere, sometime, somehow, Samuel. It will find you out, no matter how hard you try to hide it."

Sammy sat silently, soaking it all up.

His plan to make a fast, but fantastic, fortune, had all collapsed around his feet. It seemed, too, that it could have serious implications.

And worse still, Aunt Annie hadn't finished yet either!

Abandoning him to a momentary meditation on the magnitude of his misdeed, she was busily occupied searching for some other word of wisdom away near the back of God's book.

When she had found the place she had been looking for, she continued to her captive audience of one, "Now finally, Samuel, listen to this, 'And I saw the dead, small and great stand before God; and the books were opened: and another book was opened, which is the book of life: and the dead were judged out of the things which were written in the books, according to their works'."

This was really serious stuff now.

And Aunt Annie knew that it had made an impact on the young lad, so she pressed home the point, gently.

"Did you hear that, Samuel? We are all going to stand before God one day. And we will all have to give an account of ourselves. I want to warn you too, son, that God is not only going to be asking you to account for what you did with the Sunday School offering. Much more importantly, He is going to want to know what you have done with Jesus. He is likely to be looking into your face and asking you what you have done with his Son who loved you and came to die to take away your sins."

Dropping her voice down a few decibels Aunt Annie then looked Sammy Graham, eight-year old foiled and frustrated collection claimer, straight in the eye, and enquired tenderly, "And what will you say to Him, Samuel? You won't be able to say that you didn't know about Him, for you do. You have heard the Gospel message in this Sunday school for years."

Sammy tried to avoid her invasive gaze by glancing away and replying softly at the same time, "I don't know, Aunt Annie. I don't know."

Later that morning as he trudged homeward, uncharacteristically a few paces behind his big brother Jim and the others from Lisburn Street, Sammy reflected on his unsuccessful collection campaign, and Aunt Annie's very successful convicting counter-challenge.

At least, he consoled himself, nobody would know anything about his escapade except those who had been at Sunday school.

And by next Sunday morning, Aunt Annie, all the other kids in his class, and hopefully maybe even God, would have either forgotten about it or forgiven him for it.

He certainly knew that he wasn't ready to answer to God about it, or indeed anything else, just yet.

And nobody else would hold it against him.

Or would they?

Chapter Three

SAMUEL WHAT?

Sadie Graham, mother of Jim and Sammy, sometimes had to hold over the Sunday lunch until about two o'clock because her husband, Martin, was a bus conductor, and worked shifts.

In the days of the two-man, green and cream buses of the U.T.A., the Ulster Transport Authority, it was the conductor's job to collect the fares from the passengers, punch the tickets of the passengers, and communicate with the second member of the team by either pulling a string or pressing a button in the bus. This rang a bell in the cab to tell the driver to stop when the passengers wanted to get off. It was the driver's responsibility to spot, along the road, any prospective passengers who wanted to get on.

Bus conductors, working the same shifts week after week, soon came to know the regular travellers and established a pleasant rapport with them, to the extent that they even missed them if they missed the bus.

Martin Graham was just that sort of a conductor. He had been based in Ballynahinch bus station for many years, and he had become acquainted with most of the people who regularly travelled by bus in and out of the County Down market town.

On the Sunday morning of son Sammy's abortive bid for fame and fortune Martin just happened to be on duty on a bus ferrying worshippers of all denominations home from the town's churches. His was the number 18 part route service from Ballynahinch to the Temple, on the main road to Belfast.

As he moved up the bus from the back, selling single or punching return and season tickets, Martin was chatting amicably with everybody. He knew them nearly all, and he even knew which church services many of them had been attending.

The passengers liked Martin, too. He always seemed to have time for a friendly word with them as he busied himself up the bus.

Halfway up, on the left-hand side, sat a group of four, a man and three women, from the Congregational Church. The couple sat in a seat in front of the two other women. The ladies behind were leaning forward, their chins almost on the shoulders of the pair in front, chattering continuously.

Martin knew all four of them and he also knew that two of the ladies taught in the Sunday School, for they had told him so, twenty or thirty trips before.

That morning the cordial conductor asked a casual question, not expecting anything but a positive, or at the very worst, a neutral, response.

Although his older boy, Jim, had been at Sunday School, too, he was thirteen, five years older than his only brother, and Martin assumed that 'he had got a bit of sense'. Young Sammy, though, could be a different proposition. He was full of fire and flair, and could be unpredictable betimes.

So it was with Sammy he started.

"Tell me ladies," he began, by way of opening a conversation, but without expecting any startling information, "How did our Samuel behave this morning?"

These little ladies were the type of people who belong to a group drawn frequently, but by no means exclusively, from the female of the species. It is the group who love a full-blown meal of good hot gossip. Sharing tasty morsels from such a meal provides a sensational relish to relieve the monotony of an everyday diet.

The only problem for the chastened Sammy, who was by then stewing at home, was that these ladies chose to share a few choice tit-bits with the wrong person.

"Och, Martin, you will never believe what wee Samuel did this morning!" the one in at the window began impatiently, almost bouncing up out of her seat. She had been worried that Martin wasn't going to make it up their length before it came time for them to get off, but now she had his ear.

Clapping her green-gloved hands together in a gesture of animated amazement she exclaimed, for all to hear, "Samuel stole the Sunday School collection!"

"Samuel *WHAT*?!" Martin Graham exploded, missing the two tickets he had placed carefully one on top of the other and nearly punching the ear of the man in front.

"Tell me that again," he went on in virtual disbelief, leaning over the seat in an attempt to hear further details whist at the same time minimising further disgrace.

"You tell me Samuel stole the collection. How on earth did he do that?"

Both teachers who had been in Sunday School took turns to recount Sammy's first entrepreneurial exercise with great glee. They seemed to find it more comical than criminal, and there was certainly no malice in their version of events, nor, no doubt, did they intend Sammy to end up in hot water as a result of his ill-advised adventure.

Martin saw it differently, though.

He was seething at his son. Who would have thought that the young rascal could ever have devised such a scheme?! There was no doubt about it, he would have to be taught a lesson.

The conductor, who had never been too happy with people who told tales on others, was not pleased either that the two ladies had chosen to inform not only him, but also at least fifty per cent of the number 18 bus, of his resourceful son's misdemeanour.

When Martin arrived home, his wife and sons were already sitting down to their Sunday dinner. It sometimes happened that he would be a minute or two later than usual and they knew to go ahead with their meal.

That day though, husband and father didn't join the rest at the table with a cheery, "And how are we all doing today?"

Instead he just poked his head in round the door from the hall and said, "Samuel, come out here a minute. I would like to see you!"

Sadie raised her eyebrows, mystified.

Jim tightened his mouth, horrified.

And Sammy slid silently from his seat, terrified.

He knew what was coming.

When the door out into the hall had closed with a bang behind him, all mother and brother could hear was an angry voice shouting, "What's this I hear about you stealing the collection?"

There then followed the muffled sounds of a series of smacks.

This was followed by a forceful verbal expression of a father's frustration.

"How could you ever dare to let this family down by doing a thing like that?" he roared.

There then followed the muffled sound of a second series of smacks.

And finally there came the purpose of the punishment.

"I will teach you never even to think about doing such a thing again!" Sammy's father fumed, and his teaching methods were soon to become evident once more.

For this outburst was followed by a third series of smacks.

Having at last considered that appropriate punishment had been administered, the red-faced father thrust a tearful son back into the living room to the others.

Since it would be altogether too painful to sit down, Sammy took the rest of his dinner standing up. And as he stood there, eating and sniffling alternately, he thought of Aunt Annie's reproduction of 'God's words'.

'Be sure your sin will find you out,' they had predicted.

And they had been dead right!

Chapter Four

PAINTING THE TOWN RED

Summer days were busy days in the Graham home, and indeed in almost every home all down Lisburn Street in Ballynahinch.

Martin Graham was a bus conductor at work, but he spent a high percentage of his time, when not at work, in the pursuit and preservation of 'the loyalist tradition'. He held office in the Orange Order, the Royal Black Preceptory, and the Apprentice Boys of Derry. It was his whole life. He was all for truth and justice, law and order, 'God and Ulster'.

And it seemed only natural that son Sammy should soon follow in father's footsteps. In truth he could do little else, for it was all that was ever talked about at home. And the walls were bedecked with pictures of the Queen, prints of 'the union Jack', and insignias of 'the Orange and Black'.

The orange fire which simmered in the souls of the people in their street, and which had been slacked down and subdued over the autumn and winter, seemed to be stoked and poked into flame about May of every year, in preparation for what has come to be known as 'the marching season'.

It was about that time of the year, with the advent of warmer days, longer evenings, and the blatter of Lambeg drums echoing across the countryside, that Sammy and his friends began their first task of preparation. It was called 'collecting for the bonfire'.

This exercise entailed the scouring of all the local streets and scrap yards, dumps and depots, for anything combustible that was no longer classed useful. They dragged out, carried off, and piled up loads of old junk, and some not so old junk. Anything from tyres to mattresses, or dead trees to discarded furniture, was added to the stack to stand, the jealously guarded joy of its expert collectors and constructors, awaiting a slosh of paraffin, a lighted match, and a huge cheer on the 'Eleventh Night'.

Early in the year, too, the band practices, which had ticked over on a once-a-week basis in the close season, became more frequent, and more intense. It was extremely important to have all the right tunes ready for the big day, 'The Twelfth', itself. Sammy had joined the Young Defenders Accordion Band, later to be renamed The Sons of Ulster Accordion Band, when he was ten years of age. He began his musical career with the band by clanging the cymbals but soon graduated to playing a side drum.

Long before the excitement of the Eleventh Night, which in its turn was the harbinger of the happy holiday on the Twelfth, there were certain essential preparations to be made. These almost took the form of an established annual ritual to be observed.

The arch had to be erected, the bunting had to be strung from every post and pole, and of course the place had to be painted, every single season.

When Sammy and the others set out to 'paint the place', however, that proposed course of action did not consist of applying a refreshing lick of bright and cheerful, or pale and pastel, paint, to all the doors and windows down the street.

No. It was nothing like that.

Fourteen-year old Sammy Graham was the accepted lead painter and project coordinator with a group of Loyalist lads, whose sole aim was to paint the town red. And white. And blue.

In early July each year the painting party set out on its mission. And nothing was exempt. Walls were painted, fences were painted, lampposts were painted and even the traffic lights at the pedestrian crossing mysteriously turned, not red, amber and green, but red, white and blue!

Then the final touch up job, which had to be done about a week before 'The Twelfth' every year, was that all the kerbstones had to be repainted. A winter's salt and grit combined with the rest of the year's dust and grime had faded them a bit. And they couldn't be faded. They had to be fresh.

One evening in the first week of July 1967, with the annual arch up, and the red, white and blue bunting fluttering gaily overhead, Sammy and his squad of pavement painters were very busy.

There were six of them. Two had tins of blue paint, two had tins of white paint, and Sammy and another lad had tins of red.

They were all crouched down in an orderly line sorted according to colour, in at the edge of the pavement, busily painting away, laughing and joking with each other, when they heard a voice.

"What do you boys think you are doing here?" it enquired, in a stiff and steely tone.

"Ask him!" the lad at the end of the line replied, straightening up and pointing a dripping white brush at Sammy who was four tins farther down the line, doing his best to paint the town red.

Sammy heard the snarled question and the advised instruction but he paid no attention to either. He just carried on painting, apparently oblivious.

"What do you boys think you are doing here?" the same voice asked the same question to the squatting Sammy.

"And what do *you* think we are doing here?!" the fourteen-year old retorted cheekily, looking up, brush poised. He had a fair idea who it would be for they were always coming round to pester the painters. "I thought you had to be smart to be a policeman!"

Then, turning his attention back to the kerb, he continued to paint as though he was the only person in the entire street, and had the whole place to paint before dark.

"*You* are painting the footpath!" the policeman growled down gruffly.

"And *you* are absolutely brilliant!" Sammy jibed back. "I'm sure it won't be long 'til they make you an Inspector!"

"Did you not know that you are not allowed to paint the pavement?" the policeman persisted.

"Sez who?" said Sammy.

"Sez ME!" the policemen roared, towering to attention above the teenage painting foreman.

"Well you can take it from me, we won't be stopping," Sammy warned, for although his five apprentice painters had sniggered at their leader's insolence, they hadn't ceased working. There was so much to be done, and it was such a nice night.

"And what's more," the young ringleader went on, "if you don't get out of our way we will paint you too!"

"You wouldn't dare!" retorted the policeman in irritated surprise. He would just have loved to be permitted to reach down and grab that brash young brat by the scruff of the neck and shake him like a terrier shakes a rat.

"Oh would we not?" Sammy laughed defiantly.

He was the big hero now and felt he had to carry on the act to keep up the image. The rest of the boys who half-idolized him were waiting for his next move, and he didn't keep them waiting long either.

For with the next few stokes of his brush he had red-painted the toe caps of the boots of the officer who had purposely left them protruding across Sammy's pavement patch, in a vain attempt to stop his work!

With that the policeman gave up in disgust.

On his own on the beat he was no match for six of them on the street. And there could be dozens more, fathers and mothers, big brothers and sisters, watching from all the windows, as well.

Deciding that discretion, in this case, was the better part of valour, he ambled off up the street in his red-toed boots, shouting back over his shoulder, "You could get into trouble for this!"

Sammy Graham, at fourteen, had taken the lead in painting pavements, poles, posts, and even a policeman!

And this inbuilt readiness to paint the whole town red could prove to be useful, or harmful, in later life.

He might just even 'get into trouble for it!'

Chapter Five

WHY DOESN'T SOMEBODY DO SOMETHING?

Soon after the summer of the painted pavement Sammy's parents left their house in Ballynahinch and moved to take over a small corner shop in Euston Street in East Belfast.

This meant a change of school for Sammy, but when the normally disinterested pupil heard that the new school he would be expected to attend was called Orangefield, his curiosity was aroused. And when somebody told him that it been given that name because it was built on the field where King William of Orange encamped on his way to the Battle of the Boyne he began his final year's education there with some small degree of enthusiasm.

Sadly, though, the only good thing about Orangefield Secondary School, as far as Sammy Graham was concerned, proved to be its name. He wasn't interested in schoolwork of any sort and determined that he wouldn't be there one day longer than the law required.

What Sammy wanted to do was quit education and find himself a job, make some money, and live it up.

So soon after his fifteenth birthday he left school for good and became an apprentice painter, painting houses this time in all sorts of colours, not just poles and pavements or even policemen, in red, white and blue!

Although he was now living in Belfast, Sammy had left his heart behind in Ballynahinch. That was where his friends all were, and that was where he felt he still belonged.

When he had worked for almost a year, and had turned sixteen, Sammy had saved the twenty-seven pounds he needed to buy the Honda 50 step-through motorcycle he had always fancied. And being a working lad, too, meant that he could, by careful budgeting, afford the three shillings required to fill the tank with petrol.

Now Sammy was fully equipped to commute regularly to visit his old friends in his old haunts in his old hometown.

Ballynahinch was where he felt most at ease, and it was also where he felt that he could most readily press into practice, in public, the plan that he and some others were hatching in private.

All throughout his passionately Protestant late teens Sammy had often sat with his parents in front of a TV screen, watching the News. And when the terrible tidings of yet another atrocity, in the form of another needless loss of life in the Troubles, burst upon the eyes and ears of Martin and Sadie Graham, it would inevitably evoke yet another outburst.

"What is this country coming to, Sadie?" father would fume, throwing a newspaper from him, or banging his fist on the arm of a chair. "Why is there no such thing as law and order any more?"

"I don't really know, Martin," Sadie would reply, having a fair idea that her husband considered himself to be one of the privileged few who did actually know.

And she was right.

"Well I can tell you why we are in the mess we are in," Martin would proceed to pontificate. "We are in this state because nobody has either the desire or the determination to do anything about it. The police can't stop it, and the government don't seem to have the guts to even want to stop it!"

"Surely there must be somebody who could do something about it, Martin," Sadie would reply gently, but nonetheless resolutely. She agreed with him, but was anxious to try to cool the blood which seemed to be about to boil yet again.

"You are right, Sadie," the heated husband would agree, "There must be somebody who could do something about it. But who are they? And where are they? And why don't they do something soon, before this wee country is crippled?"

Little did those parents know, as they were expressing their impassioned convictions, that their son was imbibing all their genuine frustration.

And he determined that he would be one person who would do something about it.

Sammy Graham couldn't do everything.

But Sammy Graham could do something.

And he would do what he could. To do, as his parents, and dozens of other parents in the Province, had dozens of times desired, 'something about it'.

Sammy couldn't, though, do all that he wanted to do, on his own. He needed help and support.

The first thing he did was to discuss the idea of forming a vigilante group in the town, with some of his friends whom he thought would be sympathetic. And many of these contacts, who began as merely sympathetic, ended up becoming fiercely enthusiastic.

Sammy had started a snowball rolling, and it gathered momentum day by day.

Almost every evening some of his fellow-founders of the vigilante group, would bring a report of some other man who was willing to join them.

Then Sammy and his friends decided to talk to the band members about it, either individually or in small groups.

And Sammy's powers of persuasion were appreciable.

"What's the point in just beating a Lambeg drum these days?" he would argue. "Or playing a flute. Blowing a flute won't stop the I.R.A. blowing up our town. We can play 'The Sash' until we are blue in the face but that won't do one bit of good. Do you think the terrorists would be terrified of a few mousy men in band uniforms, marching up and down?"

It worked.

"You're dead right, Sammy," some once mild, but now militant, man would feel forced to agree. "You tell us what we can do, and we will do it."

Many of The Young Defenders of the band, who were now happy to be known as the loyal 'Sons of Ulster', had formed themselves into the not so young defenders of Ballynahinch.

Clandestine meetings were held all over south Down, in barns, haysheds and disused warehouses.

A local loyalist organization was being created, secretly, but systematically.

And the south Down organization was soon to hear of other young Protestant militants who were forming themselves up in Belfast, in north Down, and further afield.

Sammy Graham, because of his combined Protestant ardour and natural leadership qualities became one of the recognized leaders of this emergent institution, and travelled to other parts of the Province to represent his group amongst the others.

When a general meeting was held to formulate policy, a motto was agreed, and a common aim identified.

The motto was, 'None shall separate us"

And the aim was to protect Ulster from the threat of republican terrorism.

The Ulster Defence Association had been inaugurated.

And Sammy Graham was one of its founder members.

He felt satisfied that he was going to be able to help, through fervent involvement with the U.D.A., to keep his 'wee country' from being 'crippled'.

Somebody was doing something about it.

At last.

Chapter Six

ALL FOR THE LOVE OF LIBBY

Sammy had a second reason for making frequent forays into County Down.

While the first was to help organize vigilante patrols, which he believed to be for the protection of Ballynahinch, the other was solely for his own personal pleasure.

It was to see Libby Lowry who lived in the village of Drumaness, and whom he had known from schooldays.

They had been 'childhood sweethearts', but their love had lasted. And on many evenings, either before or after a meeting with some other hotheads in Ballynahinch, Sammy would ride on to the quiet little village to see Libby.

Since they felt that they had always known that they wanted to spend the rest of their lives together, Sammy and Libby were engaged when just seventeen years old.

That left husband-to-be with a problem, however. It was not a particularly unpleasant problem, but rather a problem of manly pride. He wanted, when he married Libby, to be seen to be able to provide a home for her.

How, though, was an apprentice painter, with a take-home pay of three pounds a week, going to be able to afford to provide a home for anybody?

By that time, though, Sammy Graham was beginning to become well-known as a leader of men, many of whom were much older than himself, and through a number of his 'connections on the ground', he knew what was happening in Ballynahinch. And especially what was happening in his old haunt of Lisburn Street.

When he heard 'on the grapevine' that the tenants in number twelve were planning to move elsewhere, Sammy set his sights on that house. He had often talked to one of the former residents of number twelve when he had walked past as a boy on his way to school, and had said to himself, in fits of childhood fondness, "Wouldn't it be lovely to live in there?"

The only difficulty was that although Sammy knew that the tenants in twelve were planning to move, the landlord didn't! And since he didn't dare tell him, either, he was forced to employ a more subtle strategy.

He knew Johnny Thomson, the man who owned the house. And Johnny Thompson lived in Carryduff, which just happened to be on the mini-motorcycle route from Belfast to Ballynahinch.

Almost every evening, then, a spruced-up Sammy Graham, on his way to meet either the loving Libby or the local loyalists, would arrive putt-putting into Johnny Thompson's yard.

"I was just wondering if you have any houses to rent in Ballynahinch?" Sammy would enquire.

"No, nothing yet," Johnny would tell him, as he had already done dozens of times before. He had a soft spot for this fiery, if persistently pestering, young fellow, but he couldn't just dump properly paid-up people out of a house to let him into it.

If he didn't have a house to let, he didn't have a house to let.

Sammy never gave up, though. And when his 'usually reliable sources' informed him that the tenants from twelve were about to tell the landlord they were leaving, he redoubled his efforts.

There were times when he was sure that Johnny Thompson must have been sick of the sight of him. He could just imagine him muttering below his breath, "Here comes that Sammy so-and-so again!"

Patience and persistence often pay, however, and they certainly did for Sammy.

One evening, when he had arrived for the umpteenth time at the back door of the badgered landlord, the relieved man came out with a smile on his face.

"At last I have some good news for you, Sammy," he announced. It was good news for him too, for he would soon be left in peace. "Number twelve Lisburn Street is going to become vacant from the end of next month and you can have it if you want it. The rent will be six shillings a week."

"That's great, I will take it," Sammy replied, trying not to sound as excited as he felt, and certainly not saying what he felt, which was, 'And what do you think I have been waiting for all these weeks?'!

The house was his, and then the work, and the planning, began in earnest.

The work, after he had been given the key, 'at the end of next month', as agreed, was to redecorate it to Sammy and Libby's liking, and to effect a number of minor repairs. This young man was determined to bring his new bride into one of the smartest houses in Lisburn Street. The by now more experienced painter and decorator was able to do all the painting and paperhanging jobs required, himself, and he had enough tradesmen friends around the town who proved only too willing to help him out with everything else. Over the space of three or four months a steady stream of plumbers, plasterers, electricians and mouse-trap setters flowed in and out through number twelve.

And when the workmen had completed all their various contributions, then both sets of parents took over and provided carpets and some essential furniture.

So when Sammy, his handy friends, and his generous relatives were all finished, the place was sitting like a mini palace!

The planning was the arranging of a wedding.

When they had agreed the date of their wedding to be Saturday June 22, 1974, Libby took over the organization of 'the big day, allowing Sammy free to focus on the ongoing refurbishment.

In the middle of the Friday night just before the wedding, with the excitement in Drumaness and east Belfast building up to fever pitch, something happened in Ballynahinch which could have spelt catastrophe for the hopefully happy couple. And it was the very thing which Sammy and his fellow vigilante patrol members of the U.D.A. had been working so hard to prevent.

Many of the business premises in the busy market town were fire-bombed.

At one stage four furious fires were raging simultaneously across the town. And two of them were in Lisburn Street, one on either side of number twelve. For long hours many fire crews battled to bring the conflagration under control, and to prevent it spreading to neighbouring properties. Like number twelve.

Since they were both deemed to have other things on their mind, the family members who knew of the fire decided to keep the news of it from the bride and groom of the following day. No point upsetting them unduly, they thought.

So when Sammy was being driven through the town on the way to the church, and saw the smouldering remains of many premises he had known so well, his immediate concern was for his new home.

"What about our wee house?" he asked somebody, and was driven down Lisburn Street to see it. 'What a miracle' he thought.

For although fires had been burning, at one stage almost out of control, on either side of their house, it stood unscathed.

"The firemen did a great job!" an uncle commented to him, enthusiastically.

Sammy agreed with him. The firemen had indeed done a great job, there could be no doubt about that.

But for some reason a fleeting thought crossed Sammy's mind that perhaps Someone else had His mighty hand, on their wee house, as well.

It was only a thought and it soon flew far away as Sammy went on to the wedding where he was joined in matrimony to Libby, the love of his life, in Magheradroll Parish Church, in the town.

After the wedding and reception the happy couple were whisked off to Belfast docks to catch the boat to Ardrossan in Scotland. They were on their way to Largs for their honeymoon.

After a journey by boat and then train, both of which seemed to pass very quickly, for there was so much to talk about, Mr. and Mrs. Samuel Graham arrived in Largs station.

When Sammy enquired about hiring a taxi to Netherbank Guest House, where he and his happy young wife were booked to spend the next week, the taxi driver asked him, "You wouldn't mind sharing with this pair of ladies here, would you? They are going to Netherhall Christian Guest House and it's just across the road."

"Not at all. We wouldn't mind sharing with anybody," Sammy told him. He was now a married man, at twenty years of age, and felt he had to behave with all the decorum due to such a senior status.

As 'the pair of ladies', as the driver had called them, climbed into the taxi beside the newly married couple, Sammy was struck by them. They were so like Aunt Annie from the Sunday School, not in looks, but in their modest and sensible dress code, and mild and friendly manner.

During the short journey, the two ladies asked kindly about the wedding. What church had it had been in, they wanted to know, and when, and how far had they travelled since? There could be no mistaking the honeymoon couple for anything else but a honeymoon couple, for every time Libby moved another shower of confetti fluttered out of some other fold in her fancy 'going away outfit'!

As he sat there watching them and listening to them drool about dresses with Libby, Sammy thought, 'These women are Christians. Imagine starting off your married life with a brand new wife and two wee Christian women!'

Maybe Someone had His mighty hand on him, his wife, and his life, as well.

But he hadn't time to even think about that now.

Not yet.

Chapter Seven

THE BLUE STAR FLUTE BAND

Although now a married man, when Sammy returned from honeymoon he continued to pursue his former interests. It would be a shame to let the additional responsibilities of having a wife and home to keep stand in the way of his intense passion for band practices and band parades.

On a Friday night in early July, when he was not yet two weeks home from Largs with Libby, Sammy and his friend Kenny Shaw went to watch a band parade in Saintfield. That was the done thing in the loyalist band-playing tradition. When you weren't marching yourself you set off somewhere else to watch somebody else marching. It was a way of life.

As they stood on the kerb, watching the bands go past, the two friends were commenting casually to each other on either the presentation or the playing when Sammy was suddenly struck by one particularly impressive flute band.

"There's something nice about a flute band, isn't there, Kenny?" he answered his own question before he had even asked it, and all in the same breath.

"Aye, there is, Sammy," Kenny had to admit.

"I think we will start a flute band," was the inspired friend's instant reaction. "I would love to lead a band like that!"

"O.K. Sammy. Good idea," Kenny said slowly, wondering what else he should say. He had been both startled and puzzled all at once by Sammy's sudden declaration. But he didn't know how it was ever going to work. To the best of his knowledge you needed to find instruments and uniforms from somewhere, which meant you needed to find money from somewhere, to start a band. And money was a commodity with which he happened to know his friend was not overly endowed at that particular time.

"But...I mean...how are you going to start a band?" he enquired at length.

"I'll tell you how. Tomorrow morning you will take me into Belfast and I will buy a flute, and you already have one and can play it. So that makes two of us," he set out to explain.

Kenny held up his hand and stemmed the flow of fantasy.

"Hold on there a minute, Sammy," he cautioned. "Firstly, you can't even play a flute. And secondly, in case you didn't know, it takes more than **two** men to make a band!"

"That's right, Kenny! That's dead right!" it was now Sammy's turn to concur. "But I will learn to play a flute, and then when I have learnt, the two of us will teach a lot of other boys to play it too!"

Kenny smiled, shook his head in amused disbelief, and then arranged to take his hotheaded mate with the harebrained idea up to Belfast in the morning.

And next morning Kenny kept his word. He drove Sammy the sixteen miles up into 'the city', where he bought himself a flute in the Music Shop in Smithfield Market for three pounds.

Now that he had procured the instrument he had to learn to play it, so he went along to Graeme Brown, a band instructor who not only taught 'fluters' to flute but also tooters to toot.

"Hi Graeme, will you show me how to play the scale on my flute?" was his simple request.

Graeme was the next one to have a secret smile to himself.

How is this character, who can't even scale a flute, ever going to start a flute band? he wondered.

He was, however, too mild-mannered a man to shatter Sammy's pipe dream, so he showed him how to play the scale on his instrument, and followed this up with a few basic lessons.

There followed, for the next four months, the sternest test of new wife Libby's love. For the self-motivated music student spent almost every spare minute he had at home, shut up in the bathroom. He said it sounded better in there, blowing and puffing into his three-pound flute! Although Sammy alleged, when he emerged, red faced and dry-mouthed after every bathroom practice session, that he was 'coming on', the longsuffering Libby couldn't see it. Or hear it. To her it all sounded like one jarring jumble of high-pitched shrieks and squeaks!

He did 'come on', though.

Even Libby was pleasantly surprised, and indeed secretly proud, of his progress. After nine or ten weeks of tested patience, the noises coming out of the bathroom had actually begun to sound like music! And by that time, too, Sammy considered himself fully qualified to fulfil his ambition.

Then came the challenge.

Where did he find enough people, either able to play, or willing to learn to play, a flute, daft enough to join a band led by somebody who was only learning to play himself? Sammy had a vision, though, and he would not be deterred, so with the help of Kenny, who realized that his friend really did intend to start a flute band, he embarked upon a recruiting blitz of Ballynahinch.

And he began by contacting almost every Protestant male over the age of ten in the town.

The conversations went something like this...

"Great to see you, Billy. Would you like to join the band?"

"What band?"

"Our band."

"And what's your band?"

"A new flute band."

"Indeed I would like to join your band. And you know Davy from Dromore Street, he would probably join, too. And so would Tommy... and Jimmy ...and Freddy..."

Sammy and Kenny's powers of persuasion and infectious fervour turned out to be irresistible, and by the end of two weeks they had enlisted enough people to form the nucleus of a band, but still there were problems.

They had people, but they needed a place to practice. And they needed something to practice on, and with.

Most of the new recruits had, or were willing to buy, their own flutes, but a band needed drums, and drummers.

It was then that Johnny Keenan came to the rescue, for Johnny shared Sammy's enthusiasm, and was willing to be practical in his show of support.

Johnny lent Sammy and Kenny two hundred pounds to buy all the drums for the would-be band, and also procured the use of the Ballykine Orange Hall, outside the town for practice sessions.

Kenny then had to act as chauffeur to his enterprising companion again, driving him to Dungannon, County Tyrone, one Saturday afternoon, armed with Johnny's welcome loan. The Piper's Cave in that County Tyrone town sold all sorts of musical instruments, and there they were able to buy the drums they needed.

Then during the winter months the task of moulding the crowd of motley individuals whom Sammy and Kenny had mustered, into a band, began.

Everyone worked hard. For everyone wanted to make a success of it.

Johnny and Kenny, who were reckoned to be rich because they had cars, ferried the trainee 'fluters', as they called themselves, and the drummers, out to Ballykine Orange Hall. And Sammy and Kenny provided the instruction.

It required patience and perseverance, but it proved productive, for by the spring of 1975 the band considered themselves well enough advanced to start selecting a uniform, and planning their first parade.

The uniform they chose was simple, and easily obtainable. It consisted of white shirts, red ties, and blue sweaters. Sammy couldn't get away from the red, white and blue. He had progressed from painting it on the pavements to having his band wearing it on their backs!

When it came to picking a name for their new band, the members opted for something simple. There were any amount of Ballynahinch Bands, Rising Sons of Everywhere Bands, Loyal Defenders Of Ulster, The Faith, and Everything Else Bands, so they changed the pattern completely.

For they named themselves The Blue Star Flute Band, with blue stars pinned on their ties and painted on their drum.

In May it was time to go public, time to launch themselves on a waiting world.

This they did in some style by holding a parade through Ballynahinch one Friday evening to a field at the Millbrook end of the town where Rev. Ian Paisley dedicated the band.

Sammy had invited the Reverend Ian along, not because he was heavily into dedications although he was not against them either, for no doubt they served some purpose. He knew, though, that the high profile politician would attract a crowd onto the streets and into the field, and a crowd on the streets and in the field would mean money in the collecting boxes and buckets! And it would also provide them with some needful, and possibly helpful, publicity, and hopefully end in some invitations to march and play at functions in the future.

And the parade that bright May evening was to end up fruitful on both counts.

Enough money was collected to pay off all their debts, and as a direct result of that initial march they were booked to lead an Orange Lodge in the Twelfth of July parade in Comber that summer!

The Blue Star Flute Band was in business!

Chapter Eight

I SEE YOU, SAMMY!

The Blue Star Flute Band was a big success from that very first Twelfth. Bookings began to flood in, and even though he was pleased that another vision had been realized, somehow Sammy wasn't satisfied.

Some who thought they knew about bands, told him how well the band played, how smart the band looked, and how popular the band was. And although he thumped them on the back and bought them another drink, what they said reached only into his head. Their flattering words made no impression on his heart.

For in his heart, Sammy wasn't satisfied.

In an attempt to plug this hole at the heart of him, Sammy became more involved in paramilitary activity. Within a few months of the establishment of a local unit of the U.D.A., Sammy Graham became recognized as one of the top men in the movement, not only in Ballynahinch, but also in South Down.

But still Sammy wasn't satisfied.

When he opened an amusement arcade, which he called The Corner Pocket, in Saintfield, Sammy said that it was 'to make a bit of extra money'. While 'a bit of extra money' would probably always be welcomed by anybody at any time, Sammy didn't really need loads of extra cash at that particular time. He had by then progressed in his employment to become a journeyman painter with Pilot Construction, a firm of building contractors, and could have met all his basic expenses from his pay packet.

The real reason, which he never stated, and possibly didn't quite fully understand, for starting up The Corner Pocket, was a constant search for inner peace, or at least some measure of contentment.

The arcade was open every weeknight and all day on a Saturday. Young people liked it for it gave them somewhere to go. The pool tables were always booked and busy with young men who organized their own competitions, and the continual clatter of coins into the fruit machines should have been a comforting sound to the owner's ears.

It wasn't really, though.

If a crammed Corner Pocket, with a modest steady profit, could have made Sammy happy then Sammy would have been happy.

But he wasn't really, though.

Still Sammy wasn't satisfied.

Soon he began to spend more and more of his extra income on alcohol. He began to drink heavily.

This, in its turn, coupled with his constant absence from home, began to put a strain on his marriage. Tension crept in between himself and Libby whom he loved, and whom he had been so eager to marry some years before. Life would never be complete without her, he had firmly believed. Now he seldom saw her, other than for a few hours between midnight and seven in the morning, and sometimes on a Sunday.

For days, weeks, and eventually months, Sammy wrestled with his inner emptiness.

Why is it, he often asked himself, that I am not content?

I have a wife who loves me, and I'm not content.

I have a good job, and plenty of money, and I'm not content.

I have helped start a successful band, and I'm not content.

I have any amount of boys who would do almost anything I said, and I'm not content.

Where is contentment to be found? Or how is it achieved?

Then he made a decision. Perhaps he should take himself away for a while. If he opted out of the pressures he had built up around himself, then he would feel content.

So one day he phoned a friend in Scotland. Sammy knew this man through his band and U.D.A. connections.

"I was wondering what would be the chances of you sorting out a job for a while in Scotland, Sandy?" he enquired.

"No problem, Sammy. I'm sure I could fix you up with something," came the confident reply. Everybody wanted to help Sammy, for Sammy was a well-known character in the fervent loyalist faction.

"But it's not just for me, Sandy," Sammy went on to explain. "I need jobs for another three fellas as well. There will be four of us."

Sammy knew so many 'fellas', and some of them were out of a job, so his contribution to their welfare was to try and secure work for them.

There was a moment's hesitation. That demand made things just four times more difficult for Sandy. When he had thought it over for a few seconds he spoke again, slightly more thoughtfully, and slightly less enthusiastically.

"Yes. If you give me a day or two, I'm sure I could manage that, too. Where do you want to work? Where are you staying?"

"Oh we will work anywhere," Sammy replied. "And maybe you could fix us up with somewhere to stay as well."

It was a tall order. Jobs with accommodation for four men. Sandy, too, though, was well connected and within a week he phoned back to his friend from The Blue Star Band, to let him know that it had 'all been arranged'.

Sammy and his jobseekers were to meet Sandy Mac Intyre in a pub in Ardrishaig, on the shores of Loch Fyne on the west coast of Scotland. And Sandy, who had pulled a few of the right strings to secure their jobs, would escort them to their new workstation.

Another two weeks elapsed in which time Sammy left his employment, and tried to explain to Libby the reason for leaving both his work and his wife to take up a job in Scotland. It was a lame excuse, something about the money being better.

When the honey coloured Austin Allegro left Ballynahinch to travel to Ardrishaig it was packed to capacity. There were cases and bags on the roof rack, secured by rubber straps, and cases and bags in the boot, which it took Sammy four goes to close.

Inside the vehicle, for the road, then ferry, then back on the road journey to pastures new, were Billy, Ted, Gregory, Sammy the driver, and Jason the long haired Alsatian, which climbed over everybody, shedding his hairs as he passed.

On arriving in the appointed pub about half-an-hour after the appointed time, they found Sandy there to meet them as arranged. A wait in a pub had proved no hardship to him.

When the four cramped and weary travellers had partaken of sufficient liquid refreshment to set them up for the last leg of their long trek, they set off.

Sandy's instructions were to, 'Follow me' and that's what Sammy and his carful of hopefuls did. For miles and miles.

When they were just beginning to think that Sandy himself was lost, the car in front turned off the main road onto a forest track. The sun bleached semi-faded sign at the gate informed them that they had just entered Knapdale Forest, not that any of them really cared. All they wanted to do by that stage was to arrive somewhere to start something.

They hadn't quite reached their destination yet, however.

Following Sandy over unknown roads had been bad enough, but the logging tracks deep in the forest were ten times worse. The dense pine trees had been planted so closely together, and had grown so tall, that hardly any light penetrated to the forest floor.

Although it was still the middle of the day, the travellers were by then in the middle of the forest, and for them it might have been the middle of the night.

Sandy switched on his headlights, and Sammy followed suit.

Eventually, after what seemed like ten hours driving, but it was actually only ten minutes, they arrived almost unexpectedly in a clearing. And in the centre of the clearing, sitting in state like a City Hall in a central square, sat a small caravan.

It was a *very small* caravan, and most certainly the smallest that

Sammy and his friends had ever seen. It was just like a biscuit tin on wheels.

Sandy drove up to this mini-abode and stopped.

When he had fumbled in his pocket he found a key, and dangling it in front of him he pointed to the caravan and announced, "So this is where you will be staying, boys!"

All at once, in a chorus, as though they had been rehearsing it since leaving home, Sammy and the other three called out, "I will not be staying in that!"

Gregory was over six feet tall, Ted was well over fourteen stone weight, and Billy was a big guy too. There was no way that all four of them could have stood up in that caravan together, without even considering minor details like eating or sleeping in it!

When they all piled out of the car, to catch a breath of fresh unpolluted forest air, Jason, the dog, made straight for the open caravan door. He was determined to investigate it, even if none of the rest of them cared to.

Bounding across the ten yards, which separated him from the door, he jumped straight in, and came to an abrupt halt. He had nowhere left to go, and since he was a big dog he didn't even have room to turn!

It gave all five men a laugh in what could develop into an awkward, stand-off situation, to see him have to reverse out, and come stumbling backwards down over the single slimy step!

Sandy had found jobs for Sammy & Co. as tree-fellers in Knapdale Forest, but they were determined that they would not be even attempting to stay in the 'tied' accommodation. Some straight talking followed.

Sammy had left home in search of happiness, and had ended up in the heat of an argument in the heart of a forest.

When Sandy eventually consented to drive back to Ardrishaig, to search for somewhere else for them to stay, Sammy left his friends to their own devices and took Jason away for a walk through the trees.

Fifteen minutes later he stopped with his back against the trunk of a towering pine tree, and gazed up through the straggling branches that were struggling up to the light, to the tiny patch of blue sky with a few white fluffy clouds, beyond.

Suddenly he heard a voice float softly across his mind. It wasn't harsh or threatening, just gentle and inviting.

"Sammy," it said. "You may run where you like, but you can't hide from Me. I know where you are. I made this world and I made this forest. My Son died on the cross to take away your sin, and you will never be satisfied 'til you trust in Him."

Sammy shivered and then shook himself vigorously.

He hadn't a clue where he was, for he was somewhere near the back of the back of beyond, and yet this voice said that it knew where he was!

It must be his imagination.

But it wasn't.

"I see you, Sammy, and will be watching you wherever you are. You can't escape. Just come to me," the voice continued.

It was scary.

Sammy called the dog, and walked quickly back to the clearing, the car, and the caravan.

He talked to Gregory, Ted and Billy, in an attempt to forget the voice which he kept trying to tell himself that he had only imagined he had heard.

But he couldn't forget.

It had been so real. So personal. And so pointed.

'I see you, Sammy,' it had said.

Chapter Nine

AND WHO ARE YOU, DADDY?

When Sammy arrived back at the biscuit tin, Sandy had returned from Ardrishaig.

"I have found you all somewhere to stay," he announced, with some degree of satisfaction. "You will have to follow me again, back into the town."

With that they shut up the caravan that they couldn't live in, and piled back, all of them plus dog, in to the car in which they had travelled so far already.

Having retraced the miles back to Ardrishaig, Sandy introduced them to their alterative accommodation, a somewhat dingy establishment called Canal House. It was by no means a luxury, or even a two star hotel, but Sammy and his friends didn't need that kind of place. At least in Canal House they would have a bed each, and enough room to change and to get into it. That would always be something. It wasn't long either before the new lodgers found a way of sneaking Jason in and up the stairs into one of the bedrooms as well. Their only problem was to keep him from barking!

The work as tree-fellers was new to all four of the men, but they were strong, and eager to learn, for the pay, Sandy had promised, would be good.

Good that was, if they had ever been given it!

At the end of the first week the four stiff and sore trainee lumberjacks were given no pay.

Just promises of pay.

By the end of the second week there was still no pay. Just more promises of more pay.

Sammy and his friends had long since discovered, however, that shopkeepers weren't keen to accept promises of pay in exchange for the essentials of their style of life, like cigarettes, beer and dog biscuits. The money they had brought from home had started to run low, the landlady had begun to appear more frequently looking for the rent, and they had no money to buy anything, or pay anybody.

All they had were promises, promises, promises.

They worked one more week in Knapdale Forest.

The boys from Ballynahinch had formed themselves into an expert, but also becoming increasingly exasperated, team of workmen.

On the Friday night they had a showdown with Sandy. They demanded their money, with menaces, were paid, and told him they would never be back in that forest. He could cut down as many trees as he liked, or recruit another squad of suckers to do it if he liked. But it wouldn't be them!

They were now, though, without a job, and by the time they had paid off all their bills, they had very little left to live on.

After some frantic searching over the weekend all four of them found work together once more. Again it was manual work. Again it was outdoor work. The job was pressure pointing the walls of the locks along the canals. This often entailed standing waist-deep in ice cold water directing liquid concrete from a pressure hose into holes and cracks in stone walls.

Their first contract was on the Crinan Canal. It may not have been glamorous work, but it was remunerative work.

There was a special bonus for the ever hungry, always hardworking, four. The firm for whom they had agreed to work proved to have one admirable quality.

They paid their employees!

On completion of the contract on the Crinan Canal, and before moving on to a bigger, and therefore potentially longer one, on the Caledonian Canal, Sammy and his pressure pointers decided to have a weekend at home. For although he was running from God, and seeking to make sense of the strife in his soul, Sammy found that he was also missing Libby and their little son Mark who was by then just over one year old.

So they came home and Sammy spent as happy a weekend as it was possible to spend, with a hollow feeling at the heart of him. And then he went back with the others. Back to the canals, to the cold, and to the concrete.

He threw himself wholeheartedly into the work, toiling away during every hour of the declining autumn daylight. It was a kind of punishment, a penance, he was inflicting upon himself. Perhaps, he hoped, it would bring with it, some shred of satisfaction.

But it didn't.

As the days became colder and darker, the work in the Caledonian Canal became even more difficult.

And the thought of Libby, and baby Mark, in a warm house back at home, but missing him, needled him too. His only source of consolation was to phone Libby as often as he could from the phone box in the village.

That was a precious point of contact.

Then one day he saw a partly faded postcard in a rather shabby corner shop. It was a composite card, but one of the photos on it was a picture of the village street, including 'his' phone box.

Sammy bought the card, and wrote on the back of it, 'I love you Libby. You will see that I have put an X at a phone box. This is the box I phone you from. Sammy'.

Libby loved that card.

It was another precious point of contact.

For the next time her faraway husband called she could imagine where he was, while he was telling her how he was.

During those frequent phone calls from the box on the card, Libby kept asking, "When are you coming home again, Sammy? We are both missing you."

Sammy's answer to that usually was, "I'm not sure, love. But I'm sure we will take another long weekend at home before Christmas."

And they did.

All four of the men had become tired of being constantly wet and constantly cold, so they returned to Ballynahinch for a weekend, early in December.

It was late in the evening when Sammy arrived back in Lisburn Street. After a happy reunion with Libby, the absent father's first question was , "Where's wee Mark?"

"He's up in his cot, but I don't think he's sleeping yet," Libby told him. "Away up and see him there."

Sammy needed no second bidding. He went up the stairs three at a time, and into the baby's room.

By the night light in the room Sammy could see that his little son was sitting up in the cot, with the bedclothes screwed around him in a tangled heap.

He immediately stepped forward, stretched out his arms, and said, in his best fatherly voice, "Come on, wee pet."

What happened next, cut Sammy to the quick.

His infant son let out a scream and cowered into the furtherest away corner of the cot. Then, when he was sure that he was as far as possible from this intruder, he continued to cry, peering out at his father through the fingers of the chubby hands which he had put up to cover his face.

His terrified expression asked only one question.

It was, "And who are you?"

Sammy was gutted.

His wee son didn't even know who he was!

Trying to check back the tears he left the bedroom , and met Libby on her way up the stairs. He told her briefly what had happened and then said, "I'm going to phone the boys in the morning and tell them I'm not going back to Scotland. They can go if they want, but I'm staying here with you and Mark."

He had been jolted into action by the instinctive reaction of his infant son, and he did what he predicted he would do. He told the others that he wasn't going back with them, and stayed at home.

For the next few weeks, up to, and after Christmas, Sammy Graham became the most attentive husband and father in Ballynahinch, barely leaving the house, in case Mark wouldn't know him when he returned. He spend a lot of his hard earned money buying presents for Libby and his little son. And he spent a lot of his time working in the house.

He washed and dried every dish they used.

He vacuumed the house, sometimes twice a day, with such vigour that Libby warned him not to hoover the carpet into holes!

Surely, he reasoned, if I stay at home and don't rake around the pubs and clubs, and be a helpful husband and devoted dad, that will bring me some peace in my soul and some happiness in my heart.

But it didn't.

Chapter Ten

SAILOR BILL

It was no use.

Sammy couldn't hide at home.

The God who could pick him out in the depths of a Scottish forest could pick him out just as easily in a house in a County Down town.

No amount of cooking or cleaning, caring or sharing, could rid him of the sense of futility which had dogged him for months.

He had to find some way out of the mental mix-up he was in, so he decided to press open another escape hatch.

Early in 1980 Sammy began to become involved as much as ever with the Blue Star Flute Band. All the boys were glad to see him back for they had missed his inspirational enthusiasm. Their wholehearted welcome for their returning leader was the latch to the hatch.

Sammy determined that he would devote himself even more diligently to the promotion of the band and the pursuit and propagation of his Protestant culture.

King William of Orange was his hero.

Pictures of his idol, in various shapes and sizes, adorned at least one wall in almost every room in the house.

In a desperate attempt to identify with something tangible, Sammy decided that he would like to have King Billy tattooed on his chest He had already a wide variety of loyalist symbols running up both arms, but they were relatively small. And anyway there were dozens of other boys swanking around all over the place sporting tattoos much the same.

If he really wanted to have peace of mind, if he really wanted to demonstrate his loyalty, and if he wanted to achieve anything even resembling lasting satisfaction he would have to go for something really different. Something special. Something BIG.

Sailor Bill in Coleraine had done all of Sammy's tattoos up until then.

And it was to Sailor Bill he returned.

When they had exchanged pleasantries about the weather the renowned tattoo artist was anxious to know on what part of Sammy Graham's anatomy he was going to be expected to show off his skill on that visit. He hadn't a lot of time to waste and he knew that Sammy hadn't driven nearly seventy miles for a chat.

"And what can I do for you today, Sammy?" he enquired.

"I know this may be a big job, Bill," the would-be client began, "But I would like you to do King Billy, on his horse, on my chest."

There was silence for a moment while Bill considered the implications of such a commission.

"It would be a big job, as you say, Sammy," he replied at length. "But I think I might be able to manage it. Take off your shirt there and let me have a look at you."

Sammy did as instructed, and there followed a second pause while Sailor Bill surveyed the surface on which he was going to be obliged to work, to fulfil this regular customer's unusual request.

"Yes, Sammy, I think I can do something for you," he announced after some seemingly serious thought. "There's just one wee problem, though. We may not be able to get King Billy and a full-sized horse on to your chest. But I tell you what I could do. I will set him on a Shetland pony!"

"Oh no, Bill! No! You couldn't do that!" Sammy shouted in shock.

Imagine King Billy on a Shetland pony! There was no way! He had to be on a horse! And on a *white* horse at that!

Sailor Bill laughed heartily at Sammy's immediate reaction and instant rejection of such a preposterous proposition.

"No Sammy, don't worry. I was only joking you!" the older man assured him when he had recovered his composure.

Then he proceeded to tell him what the tattoo he had suggested would entail.

"I can't start it today for I haven't the time," he explained. "You will need to come back for two long sessions, to complete a tattoo of the size you are talking about. It will have to be done over two sittings."

That gave Sammy something to think about. How would they go about that?

After some consideration he came to a conclusion.

"O.K. Bill, " he said. "I will come back next Saturday and you can do the horse. Then I will return the following week and you can put King Billy on the horse! I don't want you to do it the other way round. I can't have King Billy hanging in mid-air on my chest without a horse under him! Say I should happen to renege, that would look desperately stupid! Well, wouldn't it?"

Sammy did renege, however.

He never did have that tattoo.

Something happened the following Saturday which prevented him from driving to Coleraine. And then he began to think of the cost of a tattoo of such a size. Would it be worth it?

A bigger factor in his change of mind was not the expense of the proposed project, but the purpose of it.

Would having King Billy, his hero, tattooed on his chest forever, make him happy forever?

No, he decided, it wouldn't.

Sammy's problem was not on his chest, but in it.

Not on his skin, but in his heart.

Chapter Eleven

YOU'LL PAY FOR THIS!

For the next four years, Sammy Graham had no peace.

He had found himself a job as a foreman painter with a contracting company since returning from his tree-felling pressure-pointing runaway expedition to Scotland.

Permanent employment brought him a guaranteed pay packet and increased spending power.

But it didn't bring lasting peace.

The Blue Star Flute band became more and more popular, and began to win trophies for both the quality of its music and style and appearance. Although the success of the band was largely due to an enthusiastic team effort, it gave Sammy Graham a lot of pride.

But it didn't bring lasting peace.

In August 1983, Sammy became a father again. Libby had a second baby boy, Gary, that month.

The wonder of another physically perfect human being born into the world, and the privilege of being called 'daddy' again, afforded him occasional pulses of genuine pleasure.

But it didn't bring lasting peace.

In those years Sammy continued to run from God. The strange thing about it was, too, that the more he ran, the more he wanted to run, and the harder he wanted to run.

He was like the gerbil on the wheel, in the cage, in the classroom, in Mark's Nursery School. He was running away for all he was fit. But he was never getting anywhere.

In a vain attempt to quash his constant convictions and fill up an awful emptiness, while all the time trying to realize his loyalist ambitions, Sammy became more deeply involved with the U.D.A., being soon acknowledged as the Commander of the South Down Brigade.

In that position he was entitled to attend the Ruling Council meetings of the organization. Some of these meetings were held in Belfast, some in Lisburn. It was in such clandestine gatherings that strategies were decided, policies were defined, specific 'targets' were identified, and 'appropriate action' ratified.

The early eighties were particularly violent years in Northern Ireland's Troubles.

Many difficult decisions were taken at those meetings.

His position in the U.D.A. brought Sammy Graham a sense of power.

But it didn't bring lasting peace.

On the contrary, it brought a sense of endless unrest.

Many nights as he sat with ruthless men planning merciless actions, Sammy seemed to hear a voice speaking clearly to him. It sounded like the voice of Aunt Annie, soft and low, from long ago.

'You will have to give an account of this,' it said.

'I saw the dead small and great stand before God...' it said.

'You will pay for this some way, some day,' it said.

'Be sure your sin will find you out...' it said.

There was one Friday night in a Belfast meeting, that Sammy felt particularly miserable. The men around him were rambling on about 'concessions to republicans', about 'decisive action', about 'more money for more guns'.

Sammy heard none of it. His mind was on other matters.

Smoke curled upwards in wavering wisps from cigarettes held idly between fingers, gripped loosely between lips, or left abandoned on butt-filled ashtrays. This smoke then made slow progress across the ceiling like the first strands in the web of some upside-down, grey-white, giant spider.

Sammy was not aware of that either. His cigarette had long since burned itself out on the ashtray with the final twist of ash toppling off and burning yet another brand mark on the already well-branded table.

The normally very vocal member of the ruling council had lapsed into an awed silence, overcome by a feeling of abject fear. His whole mind had been overshadowed by a thundercloud of dread. When was it going to crack open above his head, unleashing the lightning of the judgment of God, which would suddenly strike him dead?

What if this was my last day on earth? he kept asking himself.

Am I in a position to give an account of myself… of my life… of this meeting, to God? he wondered.

It was scary.

The man whom all his mates in that room would have described as scared of nothing, was shaking in his shoes at the prospect of meeting God.

How could he be freed from this fear?

Where was peace to be found?

Sammy was suddenly jarred back to his senses.

Someone had taken the name of the Lord in vain.

Despite all his fervent, to the extent of being violent, defence of what he saw as 'loyalism', that was something which he had always found difficult to do. Since his early days in Sunday School, when he had so much respected his teachers, and had so much admired the reverence with which they used the name of the Lord Jesus, he could seldom ever bring himself to use it as an oath.

Every time he heard the name of Jesus it opened a floodgate of memory and released a tide of respect.

He recalled the sincerity of Aunt Annie and the others as they spoke to him of their Lord.

They spoke of 'Jesus Christ and him crucified', softly, and with reverence.

They told of 'Jesus Christ, the same yesterday, and today, and for ever', firmly, and with confidence.

They announced that, 'Jesus Christ is Lord, to the glory of God the Father,' strongly, and in triumph.

The Lord Jesus Christ had died on the cross to take away his sins, he knew. He remembered singing a chorus about it. The chorus told about 'Three crosses standing side by side', and ended up with the words, 'two for their own transgressions died, the middle one for mine'.

Now if Jesus had died for his sins, how could he use His name as a swear word?

But how could he trust Him for salvation, either?

What would all these hard men around him, think of him, if he turned round and trusted in Christ, and told them he had become a Christian?

What sort of a sissy would they think he was?

But he would have to do something soon, for the mental torment was fast becoming intolerable.

Chapter Twelve

YOUR FRIEND HAS PASSED AWAY

It was a beautiful sunny day, hot and still. Everywhere shimmered in the year's first sample of real summer heat.

It was Friday 8th June 1984, and Sammy's mind had only been half on his work that day. You needed to think briefly to change a colour or clean a brush, but you didn't need to think at all to paint a wall. Long practice in mechanical arm movements did that for you.

So as he worked he contemplated. And it was the contemplation of anticipation.

One of the highlights of every week for Sammy was the Friday evening band parade, and on that balmy evening the parade had been organised by the Hillsborough Protestant Boys Flute band, and was to be held in their town.

The prospect of a weekly band parade carried with it the added bonus that it allowed Sammy to banish the persistent challenge of conscience for a few hours.

He always arrived home an hour early on a Friday afternoon and the bandleader usually spent that extra time at home doing a pre-parade inspection.

First the uniform came out and was thoroughly brushed and checked for loose buttons. Then out came the Cherry Blossom polish and the boots were polished until Sammy could see himself in the toecaps. Nothing less would do.

Next in line, after the uniform, came the instrument.

Sammy walked down to the band hall at the back of his house and carefully removed the cover from his big drum. Then he polished if thoroughly and tuned it precisely.

He would expect, too, that all the other band members, in houses scattered across Ballynahinch, would be preparing themselves as painstakingly as he was.

So keen was Sammy to have a perfect turnout every time he encouraged local businessmen to select, then award a prize to, the best-presented member on each parade.

This incentive had proved successful in encouraging all the members to be as meticulous about their appearance as Sammy himself.

Everything, on every outing, had to be one hundred per cent.

That was why the Blue Star Flute Band won prizes!

That Friday evening Sammy heard a shout in the hallway of his house. Someone had knocked the door, and then just walked on in.

"Are you not ready there yet, boy?" came the cheery call. It was Kenneth Green, the flute captain in the band, and a close friend of Sammy and Libby. 'Dodd', as the bandsmen had nicknamed him, had even acted as godfather to baby Gary the previous year.

Kenneth, 'Dodd', was also a chronic asthmatic. And the pollen levels were high.

But he was in tip top form, his uniform immaculate, his flute tucked under his arm, ready for the off.

"Aye, I'm ready," Sammy called back, and in less than a minute they were joking out together to join the others, hot in their uniforms, waiting for the bus.

The bus was full of general chatter on the fifteen-minute journey between Ballynahinch and Lisburn. Every window had been opened wide to allow a welcome draught of air to flow over them and swirl around them.

As the bus drew in to park, taking its place in a row of others at the parade assembly point, a sudden sharp call splintered the stifling heat.

"Sammy, come quick! Dodd's not well!" was the startled cry.

Other rising bandsmen fell backwards into their seats again to allow Sammy to push down the bus to where his friend had been sitting, about four seats from the back.

The clarion call had been quite correct.

'Dodd' was not well.

In fact 'Dodd' was seriously ill.

When Sammy reached him he was clutching at his throat, gasping for breath.

As quickly as he could Sammy removed his tie and opened his shirt. Then he called out to the boys at the front of the bus, "Get the police, quick!"

As he stood there, cradling his friend in his arms, Sammy knew that to summon an ambulance would be pointless. By the time it would arrive up from the hospital in Lisburn it would be too late. Their only hope was to solicit immediate help from the police who were on duty in numbers to patrol the parade.

Within minutes a constable had arrived at the door of the bus.

When he had surveyed the scene, and saw the state of Kenneth he immediately sensed the gravity of the situation, and the wisdom of Sammy's request.

"Could you get us down to the Lagan Valley Hospital, as fast as possible?" he wanted to know.

"No problem," the policeman replied, and was soon on his handset, summoning up the car.

When the police car had been brought as close as possible to the bus, some other shocked bandsmen helped Sammy to carry the now unconscious 'Dodd' out to it.

With the siren blaring the patrol car wasted no time in covering the four miles between Hillsborough and Lisburn. Sammy sat in the back seat, breathless and broken, supporting 'Dodd' who had gone deathly pale.

The police patrol had radioed ahead from the car and an emergency response team awaited them in the Accident and

Emergency unit. Within seconds they had the limp form of Kenneth onto a stretcher and whisked away.

Sammy followed.

When the stretcher team reached a set of double doors he was stopped. "I'm sorry, sir," a senior nurse said, kindly, "but you can't come any farther. Take a seat in that little waiting room there."

The hot and harassed bandleader had no option. 'Dodd' was now in the best possible hands. Sammy had done all he could, so far. And they would do all they could from now on.

It was almost eight o'clock on a still, sunny, summer evening, and the A & E unit was unusually quiet. Sammy was left alone in that tiny waiting room. He sat bent forward, his chin cupped in his hands, on one of the six hard blue plastic chairs.

The windows were open and the occasional murmur of voices from outside, the sudden banging of a car door, or the shrill shouts of children at play, drifted in from time to time. The world it seemed, was revelling in the wonderful weather.

But Sammy's heart was heavy. And his mind was in a whirl.

There was a strange air of unreality about what had happened.

"Are you not ready yet?" his friend had joked less than two hours before.

And now 'Dodd' was fighting for life. Or could it be, perhaps..? It didn't bear thinking about, but what if..?

Suddenly Sammy was aware of the figure of a junior doctor framed in the doorway. He looked solemn.

Before the doctor opened his mouth Sammy knew instinctively what he was going to say. The stark finality of the message was frightening, though.

"I'm afraid there was nothing we could have done," the young man in the white coat said softy. "Your friend has passed away."

When he had asked Sammy one or two questions the doctor retired to attend to other immediate matters, leaving the stricken friend a sad and solitary figure, once again.

He sat there motionless, barely able to move, scarcely able to think.

Then, sitting in silence, Sammy heard a voice speaking clearly to him. He didn't know where it had come from, or whose it was, but the voice asked a question, clearly and distinctly, as though someone had been standing beside him making an urgent enquiry.

"Sammy, if that had been you, where would you have been?" was what it wanted to know.

Chapter Thirteen

WHAT A FRIEND
WE HAVE IN JESUS

When the voice had stopped speaking and his legs had stopped shaking, Sammy stumbled out into the corridor.

As he turned a corner to go to reception and try to phone for somebody to come and pick him up, he became aware of three people walking towards him.

Their faces were pictures of different degrees of distressed disbelief.

'Oh no!' Sammy thought. 'It's Kenneth's mum and dad and brother Brian! What am I going to say to them?'

As they approached him, Sammy had a feeling that they probably suspected the worst. It would be his painful portion to confirm it to them, though.

"What about Kenneth?" the father asked, in little more than a whisper, his voice and his heart both breaking.

"I'm sorry," Sammy began, with tears in his eyes. "Everybody did all they could for him, but they have just told me that he has passed away."

All four of them then threw their arms around each other, in the corridor, in an instinctive and corporate expression of grief, and sobbed softly together.

When the family asked him to go back with them to see the medical staff, and then they would give him 'a lift home', Sammy knew that he had little option but to agree. How could he leave his best friend's family in this hour of unbelievable anguish?

Since it had to be a family member who made a formal identification of the body, and neither Mr. nor Mrs. Green could even bear the thought of it, Sammy found himself accompanying 'Dodd's' brother Brian to the morgue.

When the cover was removed and Sammy was given a brief glimpse of his friend, who had been so happy four hours before, lying still and cold in death, Sammy heard an echo of the words from the waiting room.

'Sammy if that had been you, where would you have been?' was what they wanted to know.

There was little or no conversation in the car on the way back from Lisburn to Ballynahinch. All four occupants were too numb to say anything sensible. So they mostly said nothing. They just stared ahead in a stupor instead.

Sammy's first duty on arriving back in his hometown was to go straight to the practice hall, to which the totally subdued members of the Blue Star Flute Band had returned, having been suddenly robbed of any interest in taking part in the parade.

Normally, with that hall full of young and lively musicians, the place would have been echoing to all sorts of sounds.

There would have been the shouted comments on pieces or presentation.

There would have been the weird cacophony of eight or ten different flutes practising eight or ten different tunes.

There would have been the rhythmic beat of someone tapping idly on a side drum…

But that night there was nothing.

Just a total and utter silence.

The hall was full of people, but nothing else. There was an uncanny sense of emptiness.

Nobody moved, or spoke, when Sammy walked in and stood before them. All eyes turned and focused on him. They knew that he would know what had happened to 'Dodd'. And they wanted to know what he knew.

Sensing that the atmosphere was hanging heavy with expectation, Sammy went straight to the point, using the words the doctor had used to him, and he had used to Kenneth's parents. They were soft words to convey a hard thought.

"One of your best friends has just passed away," he said, tenderly, struggling to keep his voice from trembling.

Nobody spoke.

Some dabbed at their eyes with sweat-soaked handkerchiefs. Others picked up their instruments and shuffled out into the summer sunset, silent and speechless.

Next morning Mr. and Mrs. Green contacted Sammy and asked him to call up to see them. Again Sammy felt he must go at once. He would have done anything for 'Dodd', and now that 'Dodd' was gone, he felt obliged to support his mum and dad.

When he arrived at their home, half an hour later, it was to discover that they had a request. They were anxious to know if Sammy could organize something for them.

"We were wondering if you could arrange for the band to play something at Kenneth's funeral service?" was their expressed desire. "The Blue Star Flute Band was his life, and so we thought it would be very fitting if you could play at his funeral."

Sammy hesitated for a moment. Theirs was a marching band, a stirring, rousing band, and they had never played at a funeral before.

It wasn't, Sammy thought initially, either their kind of music, or their kind of scene. But he didn't know how to refuse. What kind of an excuse could he possibly make for not playing at the funeral of one of the band's most popular characters?

"What would you want us to play?" Sammy enquired.

If they had wanted some high-falootin' classical piece that he had never heard of, then that would solve the problem. Let him off the hook.

"Just play 'What a Friend We Have in Jesus', it was one of Kenneth's favourites," Mrs. Green replied.

"O.K., we will," Sammy agreed. "I will get the band members together this afternoon or tonight and tell them"

When he did that, later on in the afternoon, he told all Dodd's former friends of the family's request, and of the piece they had chosen. Sammy knew that he could have no excuse when he heard that they would like, 'What a Friend We Have in Jesus.' The band had played it hundreds, maybe thousands, of times before, both in practice and on parade.

Having informed the members of the wish of the family, Sammy allowed the men to choose whether or not they wanted to play at the funeral. Despite the fact that they knew it would be a stern test of their emotions, seventeen men said they would, out of deep respect for the departed 'Dodd'. And for the remainder of the evening they devised and practised their own particularly poignant rendition of the selected well-known hymn tune.

On the afternoon of the funeral, the church was packed. The entire community had been stunned by the sudden death of young Kenneth Green, and many had come to pay their last respects.

The band members had been allocated seats around the front of the church. It was tough for them. One of their most charismatic friends was lying in his coffin, dressed as they were, and as he had died, in full band uniform.

When called upon to play, all seventeen of those young men stood up and gave a heartfelt and note perfect performance of 'What a Friend We Have in Jesus'. It was possible that very few, if any of them, knew Jesus as a friend, but their presentation of that piece made it sound as though they did, every single one of them.

Sammy, who was a drummer and there were no drums in the church, sat proudly beside them and sobbed his heart out.

He would have dearly loved, that day, to have had Jesus as his friend. He had been impressed by the Greens. There was a stable peace about them, even when they had been called upon to plumb the depths of despair. Their secret, he knew, was that they were Christians.

Jesus was, in a very real, and practical sense, their friend.

As they stood out in the church cemetery later, in the heat of a summer afternoon, for the burial, Sammy stared vacantly, as the coffin was lowered gently and carefully into the grave. Big strong local men, and all his fellow bandsmen, stood motionless, too, the tears on their faces glinting in the sunlight.

Why? Why? Why? Sammy kept asking himself.

Why does someone so young have to die? was his question. Why does someone with all his life in front of him have to pass away so suddenly? Surely you have to be an old man to die?

There were so many questions, and so few answers.

The others had begun to file away, but Sammy stayed.

He couldn't draw himself away from the grave, from 'Dodd', and his death...

When there were no more than a dozen men left at the graveside, Sammy felt a hand being placed lightly on his shoulder.

On turning round to find out who it was, he discovered that it was Kenneth's dad.

"I have something I want to ask you, Sammy," he said, with genuine gentle concern.

"And what's that, George?" Sammy replied, his curiosity aroused.

"If that had been you, where would you have been?" was what he wanted to know.

Chapter Fourteen

A MAN APART

In the latter half of 1984 Sammy Graham was employed as a painter with the building contractors Gilbert Ash.

When the sun shone on still autumn days Sammy and his workmates enjoyed a lunchtime game of football on a large green near the building site where they were working, on Belfast's Ormeau Embankment. The half hour between one o'clock and one-thirty was the official lunch break. But if the day was fine, the match was good, and the scores were level, the painter plumber plasterer players thought nothing of going into extra-time. They didn't mind spending another ten or even fifteen minutes until either side scored the golden goal that settled the issue.

One man though, didn't play football, and didn't encroach on his employer's time. And that man was James Allen.

Even at the morning tea-break time, if the chat about next Saturday's football matches, last Saturday's horse races, or an up and coming band parade was good, nobody seemed to care too much if the allocated fifteen minute break stretched out into twenty or even twenty five minutes. Nobody that was, except James Allen.

When James Allen was allowed fifteen minutes for his morning break, he took fifteen minutes, and only fifteen minutes for his morning break.

And when James Allen was allowed half an hour for his lunch break he took thirty minutes, exactly. Not thirty-two, or thirty-five. Just thirty. Exactly.

When his workmates were straggling back on to their jobs, folding up their newspapers after a prolonged discussion on the racing results, and taking the last frantic draw on their cigarette, or wiping the perspiration from their foreheads after a hotly contested match, James Allen was back at work, quietly laying bricks.

This conscientious bricklayer had been with the company for some time and was considerably older than most of the other men on the squads. And Sammy knew that there was something different about him. It wasn't just his maturity that set him apart from the others. James Allen didn't smoke, or swear, or tell dirty jokes either.

James Allen was a man apart.

James Allen was a Christian.

Often, too, at the end of the week, as the men were dispersing to spend a weekend in the pursuit of their fancy, and Sammy was looking forward to the Friday night evening band parade, James would step up beside him and say, "Sammy, here's something I would like to give you to read over the weekend." Then unobtrusively, for he didn't want to embarrass Sammy before all the other boys, he would hand him a copy of 'Safety, Certainty and Enjoyment', or some other similar Gospel tract or pamphlet.

Sammy always took the tract from James. For he could never find any reason to refuse. If it had been someone with anything less than a flawless lifestyle coming to give Sammy 'a wee book', he had the language to tell him what he thought of him. And to shove the booklet back into the hand, or even the face, of the person presenting it.

But he felt compelled to take any tract James Allen offered, promising, in hushed tones, so that nobody else would hear, to 'read it sometime'.

The men on the site were paid every Thursday afternoon, and were allowed to stop work for half an hour to have their cheques cashed before the banks closed. Usually all the men used the permitted half hour to pile into the firm's minibus and go up to a bank at Supermac on the outskirts of the city to attend to their very vital money matters. James Allen didn't usually go on such expeditions, choosing rather to attend to his personal banking in his hometown of Dromore, in County Down.

One Thursday, however, for whatever reason, James broke with tradition and accompanied all the others in the minibus up to the bank. And it was a totally alien environment for him. The air was heavy with cigarette smoke, laden with foul language and 'blue' with suggestive jokes.

There could be no doubt either as to who was the ringleader in all the loud and lewd language.

It was Sammy Graham.

When they arrived back at the site and most of the men were sauntering slowly back to their work, James Allen came up alongside Sammy.

"I just want to say something to you, Sammy," he began quietly. "As a matter of fact, there are two things I think you should know."

"And what would those be now, James?" Sammy retorted, bold as brass. He was a leader of a band, a council member of the U.D.A., a figurehead amongst his mates, and had begun to sport a hard man façade over the very soft centre that nobody knew about.

Ignoring the younger man's blasé attitude, James Allen began to outline the two things he felt Sammy should know, one at a time.

"The first one is that I will never be back in that van. Should I never get my pay cheque cashed I will never be back in that van. What I heard in there today left me sickened and disgusted," he told him.

Sammy said nothing, just thought something… If James Allen chose to go without his pay some Thursday that was his affair. Totally up to himself. Why bother me with his religious scruples…?

The offended Christian bricklayer hadn't finished, however.

He was continuing in the same soft, but still strong voice.

"You know young man," he said, "some day you are going to have to give an account to God of all that you have just said in that van."

That touched a chord, not only in the memory, but also in the conscience of the outspoken painter.

Here was Aunt Annie all over again.

"Did you hear that, Samuel?" she had said to the penny pilferer in Sunday School. "We are all going to have to stand before God one day. And we will all have to give an account of ourselves…"

That had been years ago.

And now here was another man who had the audacity to tell him, a grown man, a working man, a family man, as loyal as they come loyalist man, the same thing!

It pierced like an arrow deep into his heart.

Sammy knew in his soul that what James Allen had just said was right. He was convicted by it, but dared not admit it. And punctured pride, and his basic natural instincts took over.

How had somebody like James Allen the downright cheek to say something like that to *him*?

His first reaction was to hit the wee man a punch in the mouth and send him sprawling, but he respected him too much for that. Nevertheless, the urge to release some of the pent up anger and some of the surging physical strength that the consistent bricklayer's confident prediction had generated proved overpowering, so Sammy lifted a large, but empty, gas cylinder and sent it crashing through the site hut window!

James Allen stood silently, watching.

When Sammy turned to face the man who by a simple statement had provoked so much uncontrollable rage within him, James spoke again.

"And you can be prepared to give an account of that too," he said simply, and began to walk away.

Sammy watched him go, outwardly defiant, but inwardly devastated.

It was hard to appear heedless, when he had been hit in the heart.

James Allen, a man apart, had got to Sammy Graham, for God.

Chapter Fifteen

A WEE PRESENT FOR YOU

The following year hadn't managed to emerge from the gloomy days of winter when Sammy had an unexpected visitor with a pleasant surprise. Brian Green, brother of Kenneth who had died, called at the Graham home in Lisburn Street, Ballynahinch, one cold January night.

He looked slightly embarrassed and sounded almost apologetic as he stood, with a little parcel in his hand, at the door when it had been opened to him.

"I hope you don't mind me calling," he began, "but I have brought a wee present for you, Sammy."

"That's great, Brian, thank you very much," Sammy replied, somewhat taken aback, but genuinely pleased nonetheless. "Come on in!"

Brian responded to the warm invitation, and went 'on in'.

Placing the small parcel in the brown paper on the corner of the living-room table he said, "That's for you. But I don't want you to open it until after I leave."

"Right, Brian, O.K." Sammy was happy to agree. If the young man had been kind enough to bring him a present, which he hadn't been expecting anyway, he could surely be gracious enough to comply with his request.

But that put Sammy in a funny fix. For although he liked the lad, he couldn't wait for Brian to go until he saw what was in the little brown parcel he had brought! And the visitor was only being polite asking Libby and he about the boys, and the band, and any other subject under the sun in which they had anything even resembling a mutual interest.

After what seemed like an age to the increasingly inquisitive Sammy, but it was in fact only about fifteen minutes, Brian said, "I will go now and leave the pair of you in peace. I enjoyed the chat."

Sammy could hardly wait to get the door shut behind Brian before dashing back into the living room, and the giver of the gift was barely fifty yards down the street when the brown paper lay in tatters on the floor.

Sammy held the present tenderly, almost reverently in his hand. It was a small black book.

"Ach Libby, look what Brian has brought me!" he exclaimed, in a tone of delight tinged with disappointment. "It's a Bible. I'm sure it's very kind of him an' all, but this house is coming down with Bibles!"

"That's right, Samuel," his wife replied, touched by Brian's kindness, but also chastened by the truth of Sammy's last statement. "This house is 'coming down with Bibles' as you say. But unfortunately neither of us ever reads them!"

"I suppose that's right," Sammy had to admit as he stood flicking idly through the book in his hand. "But I'm going to read at least some wee bits out of this one, just to please Brian if nothing else. How can I face that young lad again and thank him for the Bible without ever having opened it?"

Then, as if to emphasise the earnestness of his intent, he backed into an armchair and began examining his 'wee present' in more detail, and it was only then that he discovered that on a number of pages, verses had been underlined in red. Not only had Brian been concerned enough to give him a Bible, he had gone to great pains to make sure he read the most pertinent parts of it.

As he paid particular attention to these verses, Sammy realized that he already knew some of them. There was John chapter three verse sixteen, John chapter five verse twenty-four, Romans chapter ten verse nine, Matthew chapter eleven verse twenty-eight, and many others. Sammy had learnt these verses long before in a 'Say Six Verses for a Sixpence' deal back in his Congregational Church Sunday School days.

There was one of the underlined verses which he came upon that evening, in his getting to know you exercise with his new Bible, which really spoke to his heart. It was Isaiah chapter fifty-three and verse six, which said, 'All we like sheep have gone astray; we have turned every one to his own way; and the Lord hath laid upon him the iniquity of us all.'

'Gone astray'. Could that possibly be me? he wondered.

'Turned every one to his own way'. That surely must be me, he reckoned.

'And the Lord has laid on Him the iniquity of us all.' That is definitely something worth thinking about, he concluded.

Sammy closed the Bible, and set it carefully aside, promising himself he would have another read at it again many a time, or maybe if that was stretching it a bit, at least sometime.

It was late one evening, with the children in bed, Libby busy in a last 'tidy up' before retiring for the night, too, and Sammy just returned from a U.D.A. council meeting, where he had felt strangely uneasy, that he felt compelled to pick up his 'wee present' again.

Allowing the pages to fall open, and looking out for the red-lined verses, Sammy eventually paused at another passage in Isaiah. It wasn't chapter fifty-three this time, but chapter forty-three. And the first two verses of the chapter seemed to jump out at him from between their red lines.

'But now thus saith the Lord that created thee, O Jacob, and that formed thee, O Israel, Fear not: for I have redeemed thee, I have called thee by thy name; thou art mine.

When thou passest through the waters, I will be with thee; and through the rivers, they shall not overflow thee: when thou walkest through the fire, though shalt not be burned; neither shall the flame kindle upon thee.'

Sammy read those two verses over and over again. It was the second verse that arrested him initially.

'When you pass through the waters I will be with you,' it said.

Was this him up to his waist in water in the Crinan Canal? Or the Caledonian Canal?

'The rivers shall not overflow you,' it said. Had Someone been protecting him from the ever-present danger of drowning?

'And when you walk through the fire you shall not be burned,' it said. What about their house on the night before their wedding? His mind flashed back to the morning of their marriage and his immediate thought as he had gazed in awe at the fire damage in Lisburn Street and how number twelve had escaped unscathed. Some Mighty Power had protected his wee house!

Now here he was reading about it in the Bible.

'Neither shall the flame kindle upon you,' it said!

As Libby was on one of her final flits through the living-room, before setting off up to bed, her husband looked up from his reading and addressed her.

"Libby, I wonder has somebody been talking to that wee fella about me?" he began. "I mean one of these verses he has underlined here sounds as though it was written just for me."

"No, I wouldn't think so, Samuel," Libby was forced to smile as she replied. "He has just underlined the ones he thought were important probably."

"I suppose you are right," he agreed, almost grudgingly. "But it's funny."

That night Sammy couldn't sleep.

For by then the words of the first verse had drilled themselves into his brain.

'I have called you by your name. You are mine,' they said.

Sammy thought about that, over and over again. God had indeed called him by his name, more than once. But still he wasn't God's. It seemed as though he had been very callous in rejecting God's repeated calls.

He should respond, he knew.

But then, how could he?

He looked across at Libby, asleep beside him. Something told him that she liked his hard man, band leader, and big hero image in the town. If he turned soft and trusted in Jesus she would probably leave him.

Then there were the boys in the band. They all thought he was great. How could he tell them he had become a Christian?

And the U.D.A Council. That didn't even bear thinking about. After all he had said in those meetings down the years how was he going to go to them to tell them that he was under a new Commander. And one of the commands of that new Commander was that His followers should *love* their enemies! Wow!

He tossed and turned for half the night.

He knew that this decision was going to have to be faced, at some stage. God wasn't going to let it go away.

In the meantime though he decided to do nothing about it.

But he would continue to read the Bible from Brian, from time to time.

Chapter Sixteen

THE BLOOD ON THE DRUM

Sammy loved the summer.

For in the summer there were band parades almost every Friday evening. He anticipated Friday afternoon from Monday morning. That was what kept him going all through the working week. His great thrill was to arrive home in the early afternoon, brush down his band uniform, tighten up the skins on his three-quarter length Lambeg drum with Blue Star Flute Band emblazoned on either side of it, and wait patiently for seven o'clock and the start of the march.

During the month of August 1985, the band had been granted permission to parade through Ballynahinch, their home town, every Friday evening. How Sammy loved it. And how proud Sammy was of the band on its every outing.

By that time the Blue Star Flute Band was so well known in the district, having won many trophies for both style and appearance and the quality and variety of its music, that every aspiring young drummer, fluter, mace-bearer or cymbal-clanger from miles around wanted to join it!

So on the second Friday in August, when the band set out around the town it was led by one lad with a mace pole followed by seven smartly dressed girls carrying flags. The music to march to was provided by ten drums, forty eight flutes, and two sets of cymbals as big as bicycle wheels, one of which was played by young Mark Graham, who was following father's footsteps into the band tradition. As they paraded proudly through the streets the band was flanked by six young men, three on each side, carrying polished swords. And the control centre of the operation was the Lambeg drum position.

They made an imposing spectacle as they marched with obvious pleasure and played with obvious enthusiasm around the town, watched by a whole horde of supporters, their regular fan-club of family, friends, and fellow-townspeople, who turned out faithfully every week to follow them. These supporters knew the town so well that they could take shortcuts through side streets and see and hear their favourite band twice, maybe even three times in the course of any one evening!

When the parade was over and the band had disappeared down the passageway at the side of Sammy's Lisburn Street home the crowds on the streets dispersed to wait a week for August session number three.

Back in the band hall the musicians were sitting or standing around having a well-deserved rest before packing up to go home when there was a fairly forceful knock on the door.

The general din had died a few decibels when the man who had gone to open the door announced, "Sammy, there's a man outside and he wants to see you! He says he owns one of the shops up the street."

When the still perspiring Lambeg drummer made his way outside sure enough a local shopkeeper was standing there, looking decidedly displeased.

"What's the problem, Roy?" Sammy enquired meekly, for he knew the man, but didn't know quite what to expect from him in his present mood.

"Are you the one in charge of this band?" the businessman blustered bluntly.

"Well, really there are a number of us responsible for various aspects of the band," came the measured reply. Sammy was playing for thinking time for himself, and cooling down time for his caller.

"But I suppose you could say I am one of them," he had to admit.

"Well that's good enough for me," the shopkeeper retorted, and immediately set off up the entry at a brisk walking pace, pausing only to shout back over his shoulder, "Just you follow me to see what you have done!"

Sammy duly followed as commanded and when they arrived at their destination, Mr. Mc Master, who owned a jewellery and fancy goods shop in the town, stopped outside his premises and stood silently for a second, pointing at his shop window.

It was cracked from top to bottom.

"What happened that?" Sammy asked, in sham simplicity, knowing full well that he was being held somehow to blame. For why else would the man have summoned him out of the band hall to stand in the street and stare at it?

"What happened that!" the enraged shopkeeper exploded. "I'll tell you what happened to that! When your band came down the street the din was deafening. The noise was unbelievable. Our whole shop was shaking so much that the wife actually had to sit in the window and catch the stuff for it was jumping about all over the place. Then there was a bang and the glass cracked! THAT is what happened to that!"

Sammy was ever so apologetic. He told the jeweller that his band would never knowingly cause offence to anyone, and certainly they never intended to damage anyone's property.

Then when he returned to the band hall he contradicted that statement completely! He told the band members the direct opposite!

"We were playing well tonight, boys!" he announced with a resounding laugh. "You'll never believe it but we were playing that loud that we bust Mc Master's windy! And next week will be even better! For next week we will play so loud that we'll bust every windy in the street!"

And they decided to try it, too.

The following Friday evening they increased the volume even more.

As they marched through the streets of Ballynahinch, before their adoring supporters, every single member of the band did his best to make the most possible noise from his instrument, whatever it was. Sammy was drumming so hard on his huge Lambeg drum, that he began to feel his hands very sore. He glanced down for one ear-splitting second to discover that his knuckles were cruelly skinned, and that his own blood was smeared in tracks of red across the skin of the drum. That didn't matter to him. A few drops of blood on the drum were a small price to pay to make as much noise as possible, to help break as many 'windys' as possible. It was all in a good cause.

Then as the band blew and blattered its way up through the town square, a remarkable thing happened.

Sammy heard a voice.

When by the law of averages he shouldn't have heard anything else except the exceptional din going on all around him, a fair proportion of which he was making himself, Sammy heard a voice.

A lone preacher was standing in the middle of the square holding up a small Bible in an outstretched hand. This man was dismissed as a head-case by many, and certainly that evening he was being ignored by most. He continued preaching, however, undeterred.

And it was his voice that Sammy heard.

Above the unimaginable racket that the band was creating his words floated clearly into Sammy's ears.

"The Bible says, 'The blood of Jesus Christ his Son cleanseth us from all sin…'" were the words that penetrated every possible barrier to enter Sammy's ears, and heart, and soul.

He looked down again at the hands holding the flailing drumsticks.

His own blood was on the drum, on his shirt, and dripping on to the street.

And the blood of Jesus Christ, God's Son, had been shed to cleanse him from all sin…

The truth of that one statement, spoken at an appropriate moment, and heard in most unlikely circumstances, never left Sammy Graham.

He was a most subdued man when he returned, with the others, to the band hall after that particular Friday parade.

The band hadn't succeeded in breaking any more windows, but the word of God was beginning to succeed in breaking his heart.

Chapter Seventeen

STUCK TO THE SEAT

The phone rang in Sammy's home one Sunday afternoon in late November.

Libby went out into the hall to answer it, and within two minutes had retuned to where her husband was sitting by the fire in the living room, chatting to the boys and his niece who had called to visit.

"That's Brian Green on the phone," she announced, looking over at Sammy in an effort to attract his attention away from the great tale he was in the middle of telling. "He says that there is a special youth service on in the Congregational Church this evening and he was wondering if we would be interested in going."

"ME? Go to church?" was Sammy's instant and incredulous reaction. "You must be joking! That Brian Green is a very nice young man right enough, but I sometimes doubt if he's not just a wee bit daft. His head's cut!"

Libby's face furrowed into a frown at that spontaneous response.

"What am I going to tell him then?" she pressed on to ask, anxious to find the appropriate answer. She certainly couldn't go back to the phone and tell the lad that his 'head was cut'!

"Just tell him I'm not here," Sammy replied, dropping his voice to a soft half-whisper.

"I can't tell him that," Libby retorted, becoming increasingly intolerant of her husband's hedging. "For I'm only after asking him to hold the line for a minute until I went to ask you!"

"That's all right then, never worry," Sammy was busily hatching another excuse. "Tell him that you'll go but that I would really need to stay at home and baby-sit the boys!"

Despite her growing impatience, Libby was forced to laugh.

"He will surely think that a kind of funny," she scorned. "You, who are hardly ever in the house, being suddenly overcome with this irresistible urge to look after the boys on a Sunday night!"

"Don't worry about a babysitter," Cathy, the niece piped up. "I'm not doing anything this evening. I will come round and stay with Mark and Gary!"

Sammy glared at her. If looks could have killed the considerate Cathy would have dropped dead at once. She had just scuppered her uncle's line of defence. And Libby knew it.

"There you are, Samuel. You have no excuse," she concluded. "I will tell Brian we will go."

Before Sammy could say anything more she had closed the door out into the hall on her way back to the telephone to thank Brian for his invitation and to tell him they would be going.

There was little the hapless husband could do but resign himself to going to church under the circumstances, so he satisfied himself by venting his frustration in affording Cathy a second sustained and silent stare.

When it came time for the evening service Sammy and Libby decided that it would be pointless taking the car for such a short distance. They would just walk round to the church.

Even though it was dark by the time they set out Sammy thought that the few people who met them on foot or passed them in cars, were staring at him. Even though they didn't know where he was going. He felt so conspicuous.

And if he felt conspicuous in the darkness of a virtually deserted street his sense of 'sticking out like a sore thumb' was ten times worse in a brightly lit, packed to capacity church.

When they arrived at the church door Sammy and his wife were greeted warmly by Alex Reid, a man Sammy had known for years, and who insisted in showing them right up into the front seat. He explained that since almost every available seat in the place had been taken he had no other option.

Sammy Graham broke out in beads of sweat. His toes were actually touching the base of the platform from which the various groups of young people would take part in the service. He could almost sense the people behind him nudging one other and muttering behind their Mission Praise, "That's Sammy Graham, you know your man from the Blue Star Band, up there on the front seat."

It was so intimidating. Sammy felt so out of place.

U.D.A. council meetings were nothing to this!

The pain eased, however, as the service progressed. As groups of happy-looking young people sang, read the Bible, or told of what God had done for them, and meant to them, in their lives, Sammy gradually began to feel ever so slightly more comfortable, and ever so slightly less conspicuous. For he became engrossed in what was going on.

Although he recognized the tunes of many of the hymns from having heard them hundreds of times with the band, he hadn't known the words to many of them, and these came as a revelation, and a challenge to him.

It was not what the participating young people said that spoke so forcibly to Sammy that particular evening, though, but *how* they said it. There seemed to be an unusual peace about them as they presented their message. A heavenly radiance seemed to glow around them as they spoke of Christ. It appeared as though every single one of them knew Him as a personal friend, and was supremely happy to say so.

As he watched their faces and listened to their voices Sammy began to appreciate the depth of their love for their Lord.

It struck him immediately that what they had was what he wanted. But could he, or would he, be bold enough to set out in search of it?

The Leader of the Opposition, Satan, kept telling him that real men didn't become Christians. That kind of thing was for cissies and wimps and shiny-faced teenagers who knew nothing of life in the big bad world outside.

A battle royal was raging both in and for Sammy's soul.

And when the service was over, although everyone had been invited 'to remain behind for a cup of tea', Sammy decided to get up and get out as fast as he could. But it was only then that he discovered that he had a problem.

He couldn't move!

When he attempted to rise from the seat he found that his legs wouldn't work!

They have stuck me to this seat, he thought. That's certainly a most ingenious way of forcing people to stay for their 'cup of tea' or whatever they call it.

Then he tried even harder to rise.

And exactly the same thing happened!

His legs were like lead.

He couldn't budge.

Eventually, at the third attempt, and after a Herculean effort, he was able to lift himself from the chair.

Then, just as he had turned to Libby and was about to say, "Hurry up, for I'm going," he felt a hand being placed on his shoulder.

"Sammy it is great to see you!" a friendly man's voice said. It was the minister of the church, Rev. Robert Courtney, who was making his way around his enlarged Sunday evening congregation welcoming all the visitors who had come to that special youth service. "Sit down there and have a cup of tea with us."

Sitting down again was the last thing Sammy wanted to do if he could help it, for he was sure that the next time he sat down there he would never get up. He would be stuck to the seat for good!

"Thank you very much, but I don't drink tea," Sammy lied, hoping the minister hadn't spotted the quizzical look Libby gave him.

"Oh never mind, we have some others who don't take tea so we provide orange juice for them. Just sit down there and I will find somebody to bring you a glass," Rev. Courtney volunteered and with that he disappeared in the direction of the kitchen.

When he looked around again Libby was back in her seat, and looking up at him she said, "Samuel, will you sit down there a minute and content yourself and have your glass of orange. These people are only trying to be nice to us."

Realizing that the two alternatives before him were to either run out alone and make for home, or sit down beside his wife, he opted rather reluctantly for the latter. Then, glancing around quickly to make sure that nobody was within earshot when her husband had hit the seat beside her like a bag of coal, Libby whispered to him, "Tell me this, when did you stop drinking tea?"

The kind lady who had brought the couple in the front row their drinks had barely turned around to see to the needs of somebody else when Sammy had finished his glass of orange juice. Two gulps downed it.

He immediately placed the empty glass on the platform in front of him and growled softly at his wife, "Hurry up and knock that tea into you, Libby, until we get out of here!"

"How can I, Samuel? I have only just been given it a minute ago, and it's roastin'!" came the sharp retort. This was followed almost at once by a further puzzled enquiry.

"What has got into you this evening, anyway? Can you not just wait until I'm finished?" Libby was anxious to know.

"I just want out of here, that's all!" Sammy replied becoming more and more agitated. Then he told, not a complete lie this time, just half the truth.

"I don't want any of these people talking to me about God, or religion, or being saved or any of that kind of stuff," he confessed. "I don't feel comfortable here."

The whole truth was that one battling half of him would have loved for someone to speak to him about God and salvation, but the other half told him it wasn't for him.

Libby will leave you, that half still said.

The boys in the band will be disappointed in you, that half kept telling him.

And then there's the U.D.A. What on earth are those guys going to think? Or say? Or even do? That half kept asking him.

After Libby had burnt her tongue on her tea her impatient husband eventually succeeded in hassling her home.

But when he went to bed that night Sammy couldn't sleep, for yet another time.

All he kept seeing before him were the happy countenances of those saved and satisfied young people.

There was no doubt about it, they had what he wanted.

There was still some doubt, though, as to whether or not he had the courage to follow their example, and become a Christian.

For that, he reckoned, would require some sort of superhuman, spiritual strength in his situation.

And he didn't have that sort of strength.

At least, not yet.

Chapter Eighteen

I'LL STAND BY YOU, SAMUEL

Sammy Graham didn't have a very happy Christmas that year. Although nothing had changed in his personal circumstances, his heart was so heavy that it couldn't be persuaded to celebrate. Libby prepared for the festive season with all her customary thoroughness, and the boys looked forward to it with all their childish anticipation, but the husband and father of the household couldn't even bear to think of it!

The message and meaning of Christmas sent a chill down his spine!

Every time he heard a carol played or sung he immediately thought of Jesus, who had been 'born for our salvation'. And one evening he was watching a televised Carol Service and the words of the Scripture reading burned into his soul.

'Behold I bring you good tidings of great joy, which shall be to all people,' they proclaimed. 'For unto you is born this day in the city of David a Saviour, which is Christ the Lord.'

Good news of great joy had accompanied the arrival on earth of the Saviour, Christ the Lord.

Sammy felt miserable.

He longed to find the Saviour to discover permanent peace and great joy. For great joy was in short supply in his life during those short, dark, winter days.

The cost though, when he weighed it up, would be phenomenal.

If Libby left him, the band rejected him, and the UDA council decided to discipline him in its own distinctive manner, where would he be then?

For weeks he wrestled with it.

On his way to work in the mornings, Sammy wondered what the day would hold for him. And if he died that day without Christ, what would eternity hold for him?

When he came home in the evenings he just sat around, staring into space, uncharacteristically lifeless.

His only evening outings were to the band practices and the UDA council meetings. The band practices only served to highlight rather than ease his problem, when the strains of hymn tunes like 'Nearer My God To Thee' or 'What a Friend We Have In Jesus' came floating across the practice hall. Sammy was immediately reminded, though not that he needed reminding, that he was still far from God, and that he did not have Jesus as his friend.

The two Friday evening UDA council meetings he attended in January were a nightmare.

'You shouldn't be here,' his conscience kept telling him.

'Be sure your sin will find you out,' it insisted on repeating.

Verses he had earned a three penny-bit for saying in Sunday School kept flashing back into his mind as he sat, largely oblivious to all that was going on around him, in the smoke-filled room.

'It is appointed unto men once to die, but after this the judgement', was a verse that struck him with a sledgehammer blow one night.

The judgement! How would he fare in the judgement if he were called upon to face it there and then?

Life for Sammy soon became an indistinct blur, a futile fusion of daily work and endless mental anguish.

On Monday night, 27 th January 1986, Sammy said to his wife, "I've had a busy day Libby, and I'm tired. I'm going up to bed early to try and get a good night's sleep."

What she had been told was not the whole truth, and Libby knew it. Her husband could carry a Lambeg drum on a five-mile march, hammering it for all he was fit all the way, without ever once complaining. Here he was now, though, taking himself off to bed early, because he was worn out after a day's work! And that on a Monday too, just after a weekend when he had done nothing else but brood about!

There must be some other reason for it.

And there was.

Only Sammy and God knew the real reason why such a naturally outgoing person should suddenly be possessed by an apparently inexplicable desire to shut himself off from the world around, in the solitude of his bedroom.

Sammy climbed into his bed, lay on the broad of his back, and wept sore.

"Lord I want You to come into my heart and life and be my Saviour. I know I am a sinner and I know that only You can change me," he breathed softly through his tears. "Please, Lord, forgive me. I have tried to live my own life and do my own things without You, and I haven't made a very good job of it. Please come into my life and grant me the peace and joy and contentment that You promise to all who trust in You."

Having breathed that prayer, asking Christ to come into his life and take control, Sammy lay still, awaiting an answer.

For some reason he expected God to refuse his request. He half-thought that God would reply in a voice of thunderous judgement, "Just think what you have done in your life. And look too at how long I have struggled with you, and you have put Me off. Why should I bother with a rebel like you?"

For minutes he lay, stock still, waiting.

No angry refusal came.

Slowly, steadily, instead, Sammy found himself enveloped in the peace he had craved for so long. All the turmoil and anguish in his soul and mind melted and flowed away like snow in the sun. There was no noise, there were no rainbows or flashing lights, and there was no rebuttal by God.

A serenity he had never experienced before engulfed him.

It was marvellous.

Then all of a sudden he was struck by a sense of doubt, almost disbelief.

It can't be all that simple, he thought.

Half an hour ago I was in torment, and now I am at peace.

Half an hour ago I was heartbroken, and now I am happy.

There must be some mistake. There must be more to it than that.

That doubt was soon dispelled by a verse he must have heard somewhere, but where it had been he hadn't a clue. The words that floated back into his consciousness from his memory bank were, 'Whoever shall call upon the name of the Lord shall be saved.'

That was it! And that was all there was to it!

In his utter frustration he had called upon the name of the Lord, seeking His forgiveness, and pleading with Him to change his life. The Lord had, in His grace and mercy, responded to that sorrowful soul cry, and Sammy was saved.

The wave of doubt disappeared, soaking into the sand on the extensive beach of the Word of God, and Sammy lay back in the calm assurance that through that simple act of faith he had become a child of God.

He felt no need to rise, to go anywhere, or even to tell anybody.

All he did for that first blissful, peaceful, joyful hour was lie in the dark and bask in the full light of the love of God and the knowledge of sins forgiven.

It was after eleven o clock when Libby came up to the bedroom, and when she switched on the light she saw shining tear tracks on her husband's face.

"What's wrong with you, Samuel?" she asked, tenderly, not sure whether he had been suddenly paralysed by the onset of some serious illness, or whether he was just going through another one of these strange emotional experiences. There could be no doubt about it, that the Samuel she had been living with for the previous couple of months, had not been the Samuel she had once known.

Sammy pulled himself up in the bed and looked at her.

"I have done something tonight, Libby, that I have been considering for a long time," he began, through his tears, in an attempt to explain his seemingly irrational behaviour.

"And what's that?" Libby enquired, her curiosity aroused.

"I have just given my life to Christ," her happy husband went on to inform her.

Libby was puzzled. The expression was new to her. She loved her Samuel, but his life up until that date hadn't been the most exemplary in many aspects, and she couldn't understand why he would want to give it to Christ. Nor, for that matter, could she figure out why Christ would even want it!

The new convert smiled the first genuine smile to crease his lips for months.

"Sorry, Libby, I should have explained it better," he was glad to continue. "What I mean is, I have become a Christian tonight. I have asked Jesus to come into my life and do what He wants with it. My life is now His. It might be tough in the days to come but I am now a new man, under a new Master, God, and whatever He tells me to do, I will do it."

Libby tossed a cardigan across to a chair in the corner and then went over and sat on the bed beside her 'new man'.

She took his hand in hers, looked him in the tear-dimmed eye and vowed, totally without prompt, "No matter what happens, Samuel, I will stand by you. You can depend on me."

Sammy dropped his head on to her shoulder and sobbed softly.

"Thank you Libby," he whispered. "I thought that when you heard that I had become a Christian you would leave me!"

His wife gave a short laugh, loaded with love.

"Whatever made you think that?" she exclaimed. "I will never leave you, Samuel!"

And her husband had heard those words before in a different context, too. More words from Sunday School days jolted back into his mind. Aunt Annie had told her pupils often of God's unconditional guarantee to Joshua, at a difficult time in his life.

'I will never fail you or forsake you," He had pledged.

What an assurance!

Sammy's first fear, that Libby would leave him if he turned to Christ for salvation, had vanished in one happy moment of affirmation, and now he realised that as a child of God he would have the limitless power of his Heavenly Father with him from that night on, wherever he went.

With the sense of quiet satisfaction that had flooded his soul, Libby's loyal support, and the promised presence of God, Sammy Graham felt he could face anything.

He would deal with tomorrow morning tomorrow morning.

In the meantime he settled back on to his pillow and slept more soundly that he had done for months.

Sammy had found salvation, and satisfaction, at last.

Chapter Nineteen

WHAT'S A CHRISTIAN?

On Tuesday morning Sammy prayed that God would help him to tell everybody he met that he had become a Christian.

As he was leaving for work he said, " Libby, whatever it costs, or whatever their reaction, it doesn't matter, I'm going to nail my colours to the mast here. I'm going to tell the boys on the job that I have got saved."

Sammy knew, too, that it wouldn't be enough to claim to be a Christian, he had to live like a Christian. It had to be as visual as it was vocal. He knew how hard he had been, in his earlier day, on 'hypocrites', as he called them, and he certainly wasn't going to be one of them if he could possibly help it.

That morning at work Sammy told the first person outside of his own home, of his conversion. He was teamed up with Jim Lyons, another painter, and as they worked away he said, "Jim, I have something to tell you."

"And what's that?" Jim replied, a bit baffled, for Sammy didn't usually share his soul secrets with his workmates.

"I became a Christian last night," Sammy told him. "I asked Jesus to come into my life and now I am going to follow Him."

"Oh that's good, Sammy," Jim responded with as much enthusiasm as he could muster. He hardly knew what to say for he was wondering what had inspired such a sudden about-face in the life of his rough, tough companion. Even before he thought of what to say next he was already beginning to speculate on how long this 'good-living' phase would last!

Jim knew better than to disagree with Sammy Graham, though. Men had suffered for doing that before. He just looked across the room that they were decorating together and remarked, "I hope it works out well for you, Sammy."

Telling Jim hadn't been all that difficult. God had answered His new child's early morning petition, and helped him with his first public confession of faith in Christ.

Other potentially more onerous situations lay up ahead, however.

Driving home in the van from Lisburn to Ballynahinch, the recent convert thought of all the hard men he knew through his loyalist and U.D.A. connections. He realised that he would have to confront both the Blue Star Flute Band, and the Ulster Defence Association Council personally, but what about all the other individuals and groups, scattered across both Northern Ireland and Scotland? How was he going to tell them?

The only answer was to contact each one of them by telephone and let them know of his change of heart and life. He would take a page of his battered telephone book, with the scraps of paper stuck in it and falling out of it, all over the place, and call all the people on that particular page, every evening.

So after dinner Sammy sat down by the phone and opened his book at the page with the thumb-marked, curled up 'A' at the top right-hand corner.

First name on the list was that of William Allen, Grand Master of the East Kilbride Purple Guards Lodge, in Scotland. Sammy knew 'Willie' well for his band had led Willie's lodge in their annual parade for years.

When the voice answered at the other end Sammy asked, "Is that you, Willie?"

"Aye, it is indeed, Sammy," came back the reply. "How are you, man?"

"I'm well, Willie. In fact, I'm very well," the converted bandleader went on. "I was just ringing to let you know that I have become a Christian."

There as a lull on the line for thirty seconds or so, and then Willie Allen came back with a question, in his rich Scottish burr.

"What's a Christian, Sammy?" he enquired.

There was then a second lull on the line. This time, though, it was from the Ballynahinch end.

Sammy was shocked.

Here was a man who would have knocked everybody down to get carrying the Bible and crown on a big purple cushion at the front of his lodge every time they went out on a march, and he didn't know what a Christian was!

"A Christian, Willie," Sammy began to explain, when he spoke again, " is somebody who has trusted in Christ as their Saviour. Last night I did that. I asked God to come into my life and take it over. And now I am going to live for Him."

Another silence.

Willie had to ponder the possible long-term effects of the news he was just hearing.

"And what does that mean, Sammy? For the band, and leading us in the parade later in the year, you know?" he asked, at length.

"It just means that I will be coming over with the band, as usual," Sammy informed the worried Willie. "But I will not be going into any pubs or taking any drink. There will be no more wild 'hooleys' away into the middle of the night for me. I've changed, Willie. I am a new man now. I'm marching to a new tune, if you understand me."

There was no long pause, next time, before Willie came back with his solution to that situation.

"Sure you could do what you like over here, Sammy. Nobody would ever know!" he suggested.

Sammy laughed at the thought of it.

"Somebody would know," he countered immediately. "God, Who knows everything, would know, for starters, and so would the boys in the band. They will know that I am a Christian."

When he had replaced the receiver Sammy thought of the boys in the band. He had just told Willie Allen that they would know he was a Christian, but he hadn't told them yet!

That would be the challenge for the next night. For Wednesday was band practice night.

During that next day Sammy told some of the other men on the site where he was working that he had come to faith in Christ, and he thanked God for the help he had been afforded to do so. All the time, at the back of his mind, though, the evening to come was beginning to loom rather large.

When he had finished his dinner, Sammy pushed his chair back from the table, and looking across at his wife with a pained expression, said, "Libby, I can't go to the band practice tonight."

Libby was startled.

She had never known her husband to refuse to go to a band practice before! He just loved the band with its practices and parades. It had been part of his life for so long.

"What do you mean, Samuel, you can't go to the band practice tonight?" she asked him, somewhat bewildered.

"I can't go to the band practice tonight for if I go I'll have to tell all the boys that I'm saved," her husband replied, almost fearfully.

That argument carried no weight with Libby. She had seen Sammy cope with more frightening situations than confessing his faith before a crowd of young bandsmen many of whom hero-worshipped him.

"Well then, just go to the band practice tonight and tell them you are saved," she urged.

"I can't, Libby. I'm scared. I don't know what they will say," Sammy confessed. "I know that I can't go and not tell them, for if I do that and they hear it from somebody else then I will lose my impact as a Christian. So I'm just not going."

Libby regarded her husband tenderly, beginning to appreciate his inner struggle.

She had promised to stand by him whatever happened, and this was certainly one time when he needed her support.

"Why don't you go upstairs and pray about it, Samuel?" she ventured to suggest.

It seemed a strange mixture of emotions but Sammy was both pleased and chastened at that very practical proposal.

He was pleased to be reminded that he now had a friend in Jesus, to whom he could bring everything in prayer, but he was chastened that the thought of speaking to God about the matter had to come from Libby who was not a Christian herself

Realizing the value of her advice Sammy rose from his chair and crossed the kitchen to where a staircase went up to the back bedroom.

"O.K. Libby, that's a good idea. I will go up and pray about it," he agreed.

And with that he disappeared slowly up the stairs.

Chapter Twenty

HAVE YOU EVER BEEN TO A BAND PRACTICE, LORD?

As he knelt down at a chair in the bedroom, which was situated above the passageway leading down into the band hall, Sammy broke out in a cold sweat. He could hear the footsteps and voices of the men passing down the entry on their way to the weekly practice.

They were laughing and joking together.

How was he going to tell them his news?

More importantly, how would they react to it, if, or when, he did?

Closing his eyes and taking a fierce hold of the back of the chair, Sammy began to pray. It was a strange prayer, especially designed to meet the need of a specific situation.

"Lord, have you ever been to a band practice before?" he began, earnestly. "For if You haven't I'm asking You to come to one now! I want to tell the boys in the band that I now belong to You, but I need Your help to do that. Please help me, Lord. Show me what to say, and when to say it. I'm depending on You."

He felt slightly more at ease, rising from his knees, but another pair of voices in another pair of bodies, going down to the band hall, yanked him back to reality.

On his way out through the living room he said to Libby, "I have asked God to help me, and I'm going down to the practice. See you later."

Sammy had invited the Lord to accompany him to the band practice, and he believed that He would accept his invitation. He would never leave him or forsake him. And if there was ever a time that Sammy needed the sustaining strength of God's presence, it was now.

There was one consolation, anyway, he kept telling himself on the short walk between the house and the hall.

It was January. It was a cold night. There weren't any parades coming up for a long time. So there probably wouldn't be a big crowd of them there. He would just tell the few who turned up and then they would tell the rest. Easy!

It didn't turn out that way, though.

When Sammy entered the hall, nearly half the band had already gathered. They greeted him cheerily as he came in, as they normally did. Sammy had always been proud of the sense of camaraderie in his band, but he wasn't sure now whether that was going to help or hinder him in what lay ahead in the evening's agenda.

He went over and started to arrange the drum sets where ten or fifteen minutes later he would be teaching side drumming. There he waited, nervously, calling the occasional comment across to the others already assembled.

And every time the door opened another two men, three men, or in one case five men, entered!

Sammy turned his face to the wall.

"Lord I thought You were going to help me here!" he half-said, half-prayed, in half-panic.

In that moment of doubt and desperation Sammy suddenly realized something. God had promised to be with him, wherever he went, and in whatever he did for Him, but He had never promised that He was going to make everything easy. And in this particular case He had given no guarantees that He would keep half the band at home!

When eight o'clock came the entire band had turned up!

Band practice evenings consisted of three sessions.

There was a first practice, an interval for announcements and planning, conducted by Sammy Graham the bandleader, and a second practice period.

The first part passed off as usual that evening but then at the beginning of the mid-session meeting Sammy stood up and stunned everybody into silence by his announcement.

Standing up rather shakily, and with his voice trembling uncontrollably, he began.

"Men, I have something important to tell you," he said. "On Monday night there I gave my life to Christ. I have become a Christian. I'm saved now"

The band members were all taken aback by this declaration, straight out of the blue. They looked at each other and then back up at their unusually uneasy leader in quiet consternation.

It would never have entered their wildest dreams to consider Sammy Graham as a candidate for becoming a Christian and here he was telling them he had given his life to Christ. And the obvious strain it had been on him to tell them, immediately let them know that he wasn't joking either. This was for real.

Sammy's affirmation of his faith in Christ was the only business conducted that evening. The price of replacing some ageing flutes, and the fee to charge for their services at parades later in the year had suddenly paled into insignificance.

Sammy Graham had become a Christian.

What was going to become of the band? That was the prime concern on the minds of some of the men, on hearing the news.

As they returned to their practice places in the hall some of the singularly subdued men came forward and shook Sammy's hand.

"You have done the right thing," one said.

"It took some guts to do what you did there tonight," another remarked. "I admire you for it."

A number, however, voiced their collective anxiety. "Sure that doesn't mean you are going to leave us in the band, Sammy?" they asked.

"No, I have no plans to leave the band, just yet anyway," their popular leader assured them, and it was true. If they had only known, that he had been so concerned about getting that night over he hadn't even considered what lay beyond it!

The practice continued and the hall reverberated once more to the sound of well-known hymn and marching tunes, and Sammy felt relieved.

That was another hurdle over, and God had strengthened him. There could be no doubt about that.

The practice evening ended as always with a hearty rendition of the National Anthem and when all the instruments had been cleaned and put away in their cases and covers, the men began to file out, in groups, very much as they had come.

Sammy was last to leave the hall as usual, for he always liked to check that everything had been left shipshape. When he did eventually step out into the passageway outside the hall three of his closest friends in the band were waiting for him.

This was normal. These men were Sammy's drinking partners.

"We are on our way up to 'Hoot's' bar for a drink Sammy, one of them announced. "Are you coming?"

"No, I'm not, lads," Sammy replied. "You heard me telling you in there that I have become a Christian. I have given my life to Jesus Christ, and I won't be going with you to 'Hoot's,' or indeed any other pub for that matter."

There was an awkward silence for a few seconds then one of the other mates tried a different approach.

"We heard what you said O.K.' Sammy," he acknowledged. "But sure it would do no harm to come up with us for a bit of crack, and you could just have a Coke or two."

"No," Sammy retorted, firmly. "I know, and you probably know too, that if I started off with a Coke or two, within an hour or two I would be tempted to have a pint or two. And that's not what I want. With God's help I don't intend either smoking, swearing or being in a pub for a pint ever again. You must understand, fellas, I am a different person now, for Jesus is living in me."

His friends shook their heads in disbelief.

What a change! What a transformation!

This certainly was a different person!

"O. K. Sammy," one of them said, as they walked away. "We will see you next week."

Then Sammy's puzzled former drinking partners headed for 'Hoot's' without him. And Sammy could just imagine the story they would have to tell!

When they had disappeared out the end of the entry Sammy went back into his own house to be greeted by a pleasantly surprised Libby.

"Are you not going out with the boys tonight, Samuel?" she probed, for she had been waiting for Wednesday night, to see what he would do. His whereabouts after the band practice would be for her the big test of the reality of her husband's conversion.

And he had come home.

"No, Libby, I'm not going out with the boys tonight. And I've just told them there that I don't intend ever being back in a pub again," he told her.

Libby was impressed, but loyal wife that she was there was something else she just had to know.

"And how did you get on at the band practice?" she enquired.

Sammy laughed a short nervous laugh of relief.

"I don't know whether the Lord has ever been to a band practice before," he replied with a grin. "But if He hasn't, then He was certainly at His first one tonight, for He helped me there in a wonderful way. I'm so glad that at least all the boys in the band now know where I stand!"

Chapter Twenty One

THERE GOES MY OVERTIME!

Sammy had been right.

While he was in relating the night's events to Libby, and praising God for His guidance, the boys from the band had fanned out all over the town with the news.

It began in 'Hoot's' pub when the barman asked, "Where's Sammy tonight?"

"You'll never believe it!" his three friends burst out almost in unison. "Sammy has seen the light! He says he's a Christian now!"

"I don't believe you!" the barman exclaimed, shocked.

"Didn't we tell you that you wouldn't believe us!" one of them laughed in reply. "But you'd better believe it. For it's true!"

Other bandsmen in other bars were telling the same story.

"You will find this hard to believe, but Sammy Graham has turned good living," somebody said in one place.

"Sammy Graham has got religion," somebody else said in another. "And he must have got it bad too. Some of the boys were telling us that he wouldn't even go up with them and drink a Coke. Says he will never be in a pub again!"

When the men from the band all made it home later that evening and told their parents or their wives and families that Sammy Graham had become a Christian, they considered it incredible.

The man who was possibly one of the leading loyalist activists in the town had turned to Christ for salvation. And he had become a completely new person, he said!

Nobody could take it in!

When the shops opened next morning, everybody from pensioners going for their papers to teenagers going to school was talking about the news that was sweeping across the town like wildfire.

"Sammy Graham has turned religious!" was the hot gossip on every lip.

And, "You must be joking!" was the stock reply.

It seemed that very few who knew Sammy well in the town of Ballynahinch could rest until they had investigated this fantastic rumour for themselves. From mid-morning the doorbell in the Graham home in Lisburn Street began to ring incessantly.

Sammy was out at work but Libby was left to deal with a constant barrage of enquiries, which came from two different kinds of people.

There were the Christians, whom the beleaguered wife was pleased to assure that it was true. Yes. Samuel had got saved in his bedroom on Monday night, and he was most definitely a totally transformed character.

On hearing this the delighted Christians would invariably exclaim, "Praise the Lord! What a fantastic answer to prayer!"

The second group Libby had to cope with were the non-Christians. These were the people who virtually hero-worshipped Sammy Graham as a cult figure of loyalism. To them he was a bandleader, street painter, arch builder, and their virtually revered representative on the U.D.A. Council.

They called in sombre mood to see if their leader had 'lost his head'.

"Tell me this, Libby," they would begin, sympathetically, "has Sammy been feeling O.K. lately? Or has he gone soft or something? Sammy couldn't have turned into a Holy Joe! There is just no way!"

"Well there must be a way," Libby responded calmly. "For he has become a Christian. And he has most definitely changed."

It was the same account of the same intervention of salvation, but to an altogether different audience with an altogether different attitude.

When the remade man in question arrived home from work shortly before five-thirty, he found his house like a wake. People were sitting around chatting in muted tones, or sitting staring silently into space, waiting for him to put in an appearance. Libby was certainly glad to see him home that evening for she had been making cups of tea and answering questions all day!

He was astonished to see so many people crammed into his house, and as soon as he entered most of them rose to welcome him as a 'brother' into the family of God, and to wish him every blessing in his new life in Christ.

The few sceptics who hadn't believed that such a character could undergo such an about turn were pleasantly surprised. The man coming home in the painter's overalls still appeared to be the same sociable and good-natured Sammy Graham as they had known for half a lifetime. He hadn't grown a second head or a third leg, and he seemed supremely happy!

Sammy knew everybody in that reception party, and he spoke to them all.

He thanked the Christians for the promise of their prayers, and he told his other friends gently but firmly that he was now a Christian, and that the pursuits of his former life were now very much a thing of the past.

After dinner that evening Sammy had another stream of people calling at the door to either congratulate him or assess his mental state in light of the astounding stories that were sweeping the town. And amongst those visitors there were two whose remarks and reactions were to have a lasting impact, the first on Sammy's life as a Christian, and the second on the career of the man concerned.

The first of these men was Rev. Robert Courtney who called to remind Sammy that they were expecting him down at the Youth Club in the local Congregational church the next evening. He told Sammy that a man of his experience of life would have much to contribute to the positive development of the young people of the town and he could channel some of his talents in that direction through the Friday evening Youth Club.

The astute minister was also wise enough to appreciate that Friday night could be a difficult night for the new convert with all his former friends out in the pubs and clubs of the town. It would be good for him to become involved in something worthwhile for God.

Sammy was pleased to be invited to help in the Youth Club, and promised he would be there.

Just shortly after Rev. Courtney had left a local policeman who had come across Sammy Graham dozens of times in the course of his duty, arrived at the door.

"I am on my way up to the prayer meeting in the Baptist Church, Sammy," he explained, "but they told me you had got saved and I wanted to see it for myself. I wanted to hear it from your own mouth before I told anybody. You see I know you so well from days gone by," and he paused to give a knowing nod, "that I felt I had to double check it before I announced it in the meeting!"

"Yes, it's true O.K.!" Sammy assured him. "I was saved in my bedroom on Monday night past. I think the whole town must know that by now!"

"That's great! Praise the Lord!" the policeman replied, spontaneously. "They will be delighted to hear that news in the prayer meeting!"

He hadn't been mistaken, either. They were.

The prayer meeting had barely begun when the policeman made his announcement.

"I feel we should praise God for answered prayer," he began, enthusiastically. "Nearly everybody in this town knows Sammy Graham, but maybe not everybody in this town knows yet that Sammy Graham has got saved. Well, I can tell you that he has. I have to confess that I doubted it myself at first but I have just called at the house there on my way to the meeting and he is rejoicing in the Lord!"

An instant and impromptu chorus of words and phrases such as "Praise the Lord!" "Hallelujah!" and "Amen!" rang out across the room.

The policeman waited until the outpouring of adulation had subsided before informing the exultant congregation of the long-term effect that this dramatic conversion would have on his life and work.

"It's all right for you to praise the Lord!" he remarked with a wry smile. "But there goes my overtime!"

Chapter Twenty Two

A WORD OF TESTIMONY

It was a winter evening that Friday after Sammy was saved, and thus he didn't have any awkward choices to make. Band parades had all been postponed until the longer evenings of spring and summer, and so he was free, and pleased to accept the invitation to go down and help with the Youth Club in the local Congregational Church.

On arriving at the hall that evening Sammy was warmly welcomed by the minister who had been so keen to have him along, by Brian Green who had been concerned enough about him to give him a marked Bible just about a year before, and Richard Garnham, the third senior leader.

Being in a Christian Youth club on a Friday night was a totally new experience for Sammy, and he was very impressed by the leaders' prayer time before the club members had even begun to arrive.

Rev. Courtney explained to him that they usually had a 'time of prayer at the beginning of each evening'. Sammy Graham's heart was softened as he heard junior leaders in their late teens and early twenties praying for God's protection in the Club, and that some of the young people attending would be led to faith in Christ.

I wonder did anybody ever pray for me like this before last Monday night? he asked himself, as one after another the leaders prayed for specific young people by name.

Sammy found the prayer session a novel and uplifting experience, and the main business of the evening hadn't even started!

As they were moving out of the prayer room into the main hall where a number of exuberant chattering teenagers had already begun to assemble, Rev. Courtney came up alongside Sammy. He had a proposition to put to the new convert.

"We have a short epilogue at the end of each evening with these young people, Sammy, when we present them with the challenge of the Gospel," he told the prospective addition to their leadership team. Sammy had already gathered from the preceding prayers that there was something called an 'epilogue' at the end of each session but he still wasn't quite clear what that meant.

"Yes, I realize that, " Sammy replied. "What exactly happens then?"

"Oh we sing a bit, and then one of us gives a short Gospel message," the minister proceeded to elaborate.

He paused for a few moments to answer a query from an already busy leader about the replacement for a half-flat football and then he turned his attentions to Sammy once more.

"Brian and I were just talking before you arrived this evening and we thought you might like to give a word of testimony at the epilogue later on," he suggested. 'It would be a help to you, and the young people would love it, I'm sure."

Sammy was puzzled.

'A word of testimony'. What on earth was that?

It was obviously something he was expected to give away. But how could he possibly give it away and then it still be a help to him? And why should the young people love it?

He had to ask.

"A word of testimony," he began, repeating the phrase, which the minister obviously assumed that he had understood. "What exactly do you mean? Do I have to preach or something? And what is the word I have to say?"

"No, it's not really preaching, Sammy!" Robert Courtney laughed. "You just tell them how you came to trust in Christ as Saviour. Describe the events leading up to your conversion, and the moment you accepted Jesus into your heart."

"Is that what it is?" Sammy replied, relieved. He had already been doing that all week, to his workmates, the boys in the band and the hordes in the house.

Facing a group of teenagers, half of whom he didn't know, to tell them how he had become a Christian couldn't be any more daunting a task that telling the men in the band, all of whom he had worked closely with for many years.

"Do you think you can do it then, Sammy?" Rev Courtney needed to know.

"Yes, I think I can," Sammy said, hesitantly. "I will give it a try. I might not last very long, mind you. My word of testimony might be a very few words!"

Sammy didn't enjoy the buzz of that first night at the Youth Club as he could, or possibly should have done, for thinking of his 'word of testimony' at the end. His only hope was to depend upon God, and he committed the matter to Him in silent prayer a number of times in the course of the evening.

When the time for the epilogue came and the chorus singing was over it was Sammy's turn. Brian Green introduced him, not that he needed an introduction to that audience. Those of the number who didn't know him already had heard about him in their homes from their parents.

The fact that Sammy Graham had 'turned good living' had been the talk of the town of Ballynahinch for the previous four days. Everybody seemed to have heard of it.

As he stood up rather nervously to speak, Sammy found himself looking into a sea of faces, representing much evidence of previous activity, and varying levels of interest.

The faces of some of the lads were bright red and shining with sweat, for all they wanted to do any Friday evening was play football.

The girls' faces looked a lot less hot and bothered for the various craft activities in which they had been engaged had clearly been of a much less boisterous nature.

Some seemed ready and eager to listen.

Others appeared determined to show that they weren't. For them the Youth Club was a night out and the epilogue was the price you had to pay for an evening spent playing games or making models.

When Sammy started to speak, though, he was able to establish an immediate point of contact with them.

"It was in this very Hall that I tried to steal the Sunday School collection," he began, and immediately the restless shuffling and the rustling of crisp bags ceased.

Sammy then went on to recount the incident with Aunt Annie, much to the amusement of many. Having gained the attention of his audience, Sammy proceeded to teach them the simple Scriptural lesson which Aunt Annie had taught him.

It was, 'Be sure your sin will find you out'.

For the next ten minutes the young people who had often proved fidgety on previous occasions, listened intently to their new leader as he gave them his 'word of testimony' focussing particular on incidents of local interest. There was the story of the setting up of the Blue Star Flute Band, the preacher in the square, and his salvation four nights before in his bedroom in Lisburn Street.

Before finishing Sammy challenged the young people to trust His Saviour, Whom he had discovered to be the sole source of peace, joy and satisfaction in life.

As they were leaving the hall in small and even slightly subdued groups at the end of the epilogue, some of the young people came up to Sammy and asked, "Will you come back again next week, Mister?"

"Yes, I will," he promised.

Although he couldn't have been aware of it at the time, that night was to mark the beginning of a long, happy and rewarding association with the Youth Club in his church.

He hadn't been many months in youth work until Brian and Richard recognised his ability for working with teenagers and recommended him to Jimmy Mc Clenaghan, the Captain of the Boys' Brigade.

Immediately following that Jimmy approached the enthusiastic new Christian to ask him to become a B.B. leader. Sammy was happy to be involved and was sent off to a training course in the Centre in Rathmore House, Larne.

Sammy soon realized that he loved the work in the Boy's brigade. He found the need to study the Scriptures in order to prepare for talking to the boys about spiritual matters helpful, but above all he seized every possible opportunity to tell them how faith in Christ had changed his life.

He gave his first 'word of testimony' in the Youth Club in Ballynahinch Congregational Church on Friday 1st February, 1986, but Sammy has told hundreds of people, both young and old, in that same church that same enthralling story of salvation ever since.

Chapter Twenty Three

WHERE ARE THEY?

Perhaps the sternest test both of Sammy's faith and his resolve came the following week at the local branch meeting of the Ulster Defence Association in Ballynahinch.

Again he had told Libby on his way out that he was 'going to nail his colours to the mast' there. He had prayed a lot about it, asking for God's help and protection, for he was not looking forward to it.

When everybody had gathered and the chairman had just begun to introduce the first item for discussion, Sammy interrupted him.

"Before you go any further," he cut in, "I have something important to tell you all. I won't be back here."

There was an uncomfortable silence for a minute or two.

Some of the men around the table shuffled uneasily, for they had heard the rumours that had been circulating in the town, but weren't sure if they could possibly be true. And if by some chance there was any truth in them, how would they affect Sammy's position in their organisation?

Now they had their answer.

"What to you mean you won't be back?" someone asked incredulously after a bit. It had taken them all some time to appreciate the possible consequences of such a decision.

Sammy Graham, one of their key men, was talking about leaving!

"I won't be coming back because I'm a Christian now and that means I cannot remain a member of this organisation," he endeavoured to explain. "The Ulster Defence Association doesn't honour God, and I now belong to God. I have handed my life over to Him."

There was a second period of smoke-filled silence as everybody struggled to come to terms with the ramifications of Sammy's shock announcement.

"Don't worry about that!" the chairman argued. "You can still stay with us. We need your wealth of experience. You don't have to leave just because you are a Christian, Sammy. Sure there are some Christians in the U.D.A."

This declaration was accompanied by knowing nods from some of the other men in the meeting.

"Are there indeed? That is certainly news to me," Sammy countered immediately. "Just as a matter of interest could you please tell me who they are and where they are? I have been a member of the U.D.A. for more than ten years now and in that time I have sat in Council meetings at the very highest level all over this Province. I have to tell you, though, that in all that time I have never met a Christian in the organization."

Faced with nothing more than a row of blank, unresponsive stares, Sammy went on to qualify his former statement. "At least if there are Christians in the U.D.A. none of them ever told me about Jesus Christ, and that God loves me and sent His Son to the cross of Calvary to die for me. For those ten years nobody in any U.D.A. meeting anywhere ever told me that I was a sinner and that I needed to be saved."

When they realized that Sammy meant what he said and that it would be difficult to persuade him to change his mind, another man who hadn't previously spoken asked, "What made you suddenly come to this decision to become a Christian, Sammy?"

Relieved that the committee members hadn't turned nasty, but rather seemed inquisitive, Sammy was glad of the opportunity to inform these men who had been his friends for years, what had made him come to the decision to turn to Christ for salvation.

It had opened the way for him to give another 'word of testimony'.

"You will probably be surprised to hear that it wasn't a sudden decision on my part to become a Christian," he told the curious, but still rather confused group. "I have been thinking about this for a long time. And by that I mean for years. There were times when I sat here with you men and realized that I would have to give an account to God of all that I have said and done. I struggled with it, and hoped it would go away, but it didn't. It just got worse until I couldn't live with it. Then on Monday night of last week I gave my life to Christ, and I intend to follow and serve Him as best I can, and with His help."

By the time Sammy had finished the men in the room had a much clearer picture of where he stood and of his firm determination to leave the organization. It would be pointless to persist in trying to persuade him otherwise.

Sammy rose from his seat and said, "I might as well be going now, fellas."

He then went round the room and shook every man's hand and they all without exception wished him 'All the best!" A few of them even added, "And thanks for all you have done for us."

As he crossed to the door Sammy was amazed to see that some of the other men in the room were pulling on their coats and preparing to follow him out into the winter night.

Sammy Graham was leaving for good and all business for that evening had been suspended.

Not long after he reached home Sammy lifted his heart in thanksgiving to God for His protecting care. Things could have proved awkward for him at that meeting, but they hadn't. God had seen to that.

A few days later, his bountiful Heavenly Father had a further bonus in store for the new Christian who was determined to live for Him.

Just before Christmas the previous year, and certainly well before his conversion in late January, Sammy and a friend, Jim Lyons, had tendered for a big painting job in Lisburn. It was their intention if they were awarded the job, to 'go out on their own'. They would set up their own painting and decorating business.

Now within days of trusting in Christ Sammy took a phone call one day to be told that they had been awarded the contract.

He and his partner were to paint one hundred and eighty houses on a new private development in Lisburn to start with. And there would be further jobs to come if their workmanship proved to be up to standard.

Sammy was pleased.

He felt in a strange way that God had taken over his life, and was organizing his affairs. He and Jim hadn't been very hopeful of obtaining that contract for they had been aware that they were competing with a number of much larger outfits.

But God had His hand on His child.

A few months later, when the job in Lisburn was well under way, and invitations were coming in to submit prices for yet more work, Jim Lyons realized that being a manager was not for him. He would much rather be a painter than a partner so the two men agreed that Sammy should take over the management of the business and Jim would happily revert to being his employee.

The God who had saved Sammy Graham had also undertaken to see him set up in business.

On reflecting upon God's kindness to him and dealings in his life sometime later Sammy was pleased to discover a verse that Rev. Courtney quoted one Sunday morning in Church. He had heard it before but on that particular morning it came home with a new meaning for the grateful new Christian.

That afternoon he underlined it in his own Bible.

'Them that honour me I will honour', it said.

Chapter Twenty Four

PRAISE THE LORD!

It was on a Saturday evening almost two weeks after his conversion that Sammy was standing looking out the window of his Lisburn Street home. He was watching a number of his former drinking associates laughed and joked as they entered the two pubs across the road.

What amazed him was that although he had been in The Stag's Head and Grace Smylie's hundreds of times before, he had no desire whatsoever to go into either of them, or indeed any other pub for that matter, now.

Sammy Graham had been totally transformed and was happier than he had ever been. It was virtually unbelievable what God had done in his life!

As he stood there he saw a man in Salvation Army uniform coming down the street. He was making his way along to the two pubs with 'The War Cry', a pamphlet which he distributed to all the occupants of all the pubs in Ballynahinch.

Although he didn't know his name, Sammy knew the man to see. He was one of a faithful team of both men and women who took it in turns, singly or in pairs, to visit the bars in the town on a Saturday night.

The one-time regular drinker was well aware, too, of some of the good-natured banter and not so good natured mockery that these dedicated War Cry distributors often faced. For some strange reason, though, Sammy had always secretly respected them. Perhaps it was that they reminded him of his childhood days and Aunt Annie with her inescapable pronouncement, 'be sure your sin will find you out', but he could never tear up a tract defiantly before them, or crumple it up and throw it back in their faces as he had seen done so often. Sammy had been less able to oppose these people than some of his mates because deep in the heart and soul of him he knew that they were right. What was more, they had what he had very much coveted, peace of mind and soul. So he usually shoved whatever they gave him into his pocket and occasionally even glanced over it before tossing it into the fire at home.

As the man in the uniform came closer, Sammy felt compelled to go out and encourage him. He certainly wouldn't get much of a lift where he was going, yet he deserved some commendation for his tenacious commitment to the cause of Christ.

Sammy stepped out of the house on a raw February night and met the Salvation Army man outside Jackie Brown's hardware shop.

"Hello there mister," he said, holding up his hand like a policeman on point duty, and the pedestrian with the pile of pamphlets in one hand and collecting box in the other, stopped before him. Although he wasn't sure what to expect from this unexpected encounter the man in the Salvation Army overcoat and cap afforded Sammy a faint smile of recognition, for he had encountered the bandleader from Lisburn Street in many a pub before.

Before he had any more time to wonder what this was all about Sammy went on to inform him.

"There is something I thought I ought to tell you, and I'm quite sure you will be pleased to hear it," he began.

"And what's that?" the man asked in surprise.

"You probably know me, for you must have seen me in some pub or other on a Saturday night," Sammy went on to explain to further warmer smiles from his listener. These signified, whether intentionally or otherwise, a growing sense of recognition.

"I just want you to know that I trusted in Christ as my Saviour nearly a fortnight ago, and am completely changed. I am now a new creation in Christ Jesus" the recent convert said.

"Well, praise the Lord!" the Salvation Army worker shouted out at once. "That's great!"

"I knew you would think so," Sammy replied, giving the still somewhat astonished Gospel messenger a friendly pat on the shoulder. "Just keep on doing what you are doing! God will bless you!"

"Thank you! And don't worry, I will!" came the hearty response.

After almost ten minutes of friendly conversation they parted, promising to pray for each other. Sammy was glad to be making his way back towards home again for he had gone out without a coat and the chill of the winter night was beginning to penetrate right through to his bones.

When he was just about to go in through his own front door he turned for a final glance back across the street, and what he saw gave him a marvellous sense of satisfaction. The man with 'The War Cry' was disappearing eagerly, almost aggressively, in through the door of 'The Stag's Head'! What he had just learnt from a new and enthusiastic Christian had sent him about his business with a spring in his step and a renewed faith in the power of God to work miracles in Ballynahinch.

Sammy stood silently for a moment, motionless, statuesque.

A name had shot into his mind like a bolt from the blue!

The name was James Allen.

If hearing of his conversion had so thrilled the Salvation Army man who didn't know him, what would it not do to James Allen who did? he wondered immediately.

James Allen who had been so faithful in his testimony and witness.

James Allen who had given Sammy Graham and every other tradesman on whatever site he happened to be working, a Gospel tract without fail every Thursday when they had all been brought together to be paid.

And James Allen who had so fearlessly confronted Sammy with the truth that he was one day going to have to give an account to God of all that he had done, and said, in this life.

It was imperative that he told that quiet but committed personal evangelist that he was now a believer.

When he had warmed himself sufficiently at the fire to feel comfortable again, Sammy began to leaf through the telephone directory. He thought that James Allen lived somewhere in the Dromore or Banbridge areas of County Down but he had no idea of his address.

On discovering that there were ninety-three J. Allens in the directory Sammy began to ring all those who he thought could possibly be his man.

"Hello, sorry to trouble you, but does James Allen, who used to work as a bricklayer for Gilbert Ash live there?" was his stock opening question to whoever answered his call.

It was mostly a woman's voice that would come back with something like, "No. Sorry. I'm afraid you must have got the wrong Allen. My husband is John...or Joseph...or..."

Once it was a young man who replied jauntily, "Sorry, mate. We have no bricklayers here!"

The sixth call, though, proved more promising.

Just when Sammy had begun to fear that he was fast running out of fairly likely J. Allens, the response to his initial enquiry came back in a voice he thought he recognised. It was slightly gruffer than he imagined it would be, but it was certainly hopeful.

"Yes. That's me," it said simply.

"You will probably remember me, James," Sammy proceeded to tell the man at the other end of the line. "This is Sammy Graham. I was a painter with Gilbert Ash and you used to give us tracts every pay day."

"Yes. I know who you are, O.K.," James replied. "I'm sure I will never forget you for you were not an easy man to speak to about your soul."

"You are right. I wasn't'" the slightly chastened Sammy conceded. "But I thought you might be interested to know that I have got saved, nearly two weeks ago."

Silence descended upon the line.

Sammy thought that James Allen had rung off.

But no. He hadn't.

He had just started to sob softly.

"Praise the Lord!" he whispered hoarsely, eventually. "Praise the Lord."

The tenderness in the older man touched Sammy and he began to weep as well.

When James Allen had regained sufficient composure to make any prolonged comment, he volunteered some intriguing information.

"You know, Sammy," he said, "I have been praying for you since the day I was sure you were going to hit me. You remember the time I mean? The day you put the gas tank through the site hut window… And now God has answered my prayer. Praise His Name!"

"Thank you James for your witness and your prayers," Sammy responded in hushed, humbled tones

"And praise the Lord for men like you!"

Chapter Twenty Five

I'M NOT SURPRISED, SAMUEL

"Hello, Samuel, how are you?" Peggy George greeted her former neighbour in friendly fashion late one afternoon in the Main Street of their home town.

Sammy had known Peggy and her sister Mary for years for they had lived a long time in Lisburn Street a few doors along from his home. Their father, who was affectionately known to everybody as 'Granda Totten', was a much-loved character in the district.

Not only did Sammy know the Totten family well, but he also knew that Mary and Peggy were Christians, and had been for years.

"I'm doing fine, Peggy," he responded whole-heartedly to her kind enquiry after his health. "In fact I'm doing great. Have you not heard that I became a Christian a week or two back, one Monday night?"

Peggy appeared pleased.

"No, Samuel. I hadn't heard, but I am delighted," she replied.

Then before Sammy had time to make any reply she went on to add, "I'm delighted, but I'm not surprised, Samuel."

What a strange statement!

Sammy was startled.

Virtually everybody who had heard that Sammy Graham had got saved, or turned good living, as some chose to call his life-transforming experience, had been totally taken aback, almost to the point of disbelief. And here was a woman, standing in front of him in the street, telling him that she wasn't at all surprised that he had come to Christ!

A puzzled look crossed Sammy's face and he asked the question which immediately sprang to his lips. "How could you not be surprised at my salvation, Peggy? Nobody knows any better than you, the godless, hopeless hoodlum I have been!"

"That's true, " Peggy felt it best to shed more light on the comment which had so confused her erstwhile neighbour. "Nobody knows you much better than me, but we have been praying for you every Friday night out in out wee prayer meeting in Magheraknock Mission Hall. Indeed we have been making Samuel Graham a special prayer focus every Friday night for years."

She paused and then added with a broad grin, "And God answers prayer."

Sammy was stupefied.

He knew the little Mission Hall Peggy was talking about. He had passed it often and wondered why anybody would ever want to worship in such a place. To him it looked nothing more than a corrugated iron hut strategically situated at the absolute heart of Nowhere.

Yet the people there had been praying for him!

Every Friday night!

And that explained something else!

It was small wonder that he had felt so uncomfortable so often in the U.D.A. Council meetings.

For they had been on a Friday night!

When he had been sitting restlessly in those meetings some sincere Christians in a tin hut miles away had been making him 'a special focus for prayer'.

Although Peggy hadn't been surprised to learn of Sammy's salvation in answer to those fervent and persistent prayers he had been surprised to learn of the Magheraknock prayer meetings. And an even bigger surprise was in store for him when Kenneth Green, senior, father of the lad who had died at the band parade, told Sammy that a lady called Moy Leahy wanted to meet him.

Kenneth informed Sammy that he would send Moy round to his home sometime for he would definitely be interested in the story she had to tell.

He must have acted quickly, too, for within a few days a woman that Sammy had seen so often standing as a spectator at band parades, knocked on his door.

"I'm Moy Leahy," the visitor said. "Kenneth Green told me to call round and introduce myself to you."

"Sure I almost feel I know you!" Sammy exclaimed at once. "You are the woman who has been coming to all our band parades for months. Maybe even for years!"

"That's right. I have," Moy replied, briefly, without committing herself.

"Come on in then," Sammy invited, always willing to welcome a loyal supporter of the Blue Star Flute Band.

As Moy found a seat in the small living room Sammy laughed as he told her, "I used to say to the boys in the band that if Ulster had a lot more women like you we would have nothing to fear! I remember seeing you standing freezing and alone last winter in Newtownards when we were daft enough to march on through the snow!"

It was then the lady's turn to laugh but she did so rather shyly, for she had a message on her mind. The purpose of her visit to Sammy's home was to explain the purpose of her presence at all the outings of the Blue Star Flute Band.

"Thank you, Sammy'" she replied, slightly embarrassed at his obvious recognition of her perceived loyalty. "I have come here tonight, though, to let you know just exactly why I was at all those parades. Your music was good, and your turnout excellent, don't get me wrong, but I didn't follow you all over the country just to see the band marching or hear it playing."

"Well why were you there then?" Sammy was at a loss to know.

Moy settled back more comfortably into the seat she had selected, and began.

"The story starts a few years ago," she explained, "just after young Kenneth Green died on the way to the parade in Hillsborough. After his funeral his parents asked me, and I use their own words, 'to pray for a fella called Sammy Graham. He runs the Blue Star Flute Band and you can't miss him for he beats the big drum in it!'"

Sammy sat mesmerised.

Was this another one of these 'we've been praying for you' type stories about to unfold?

"So that is why I have been to all your band parades, Sammy," Moy went on. "When you were passing me, hammering your big drum 'til the sweat rolled off you, I was standing on the footpath watching you, and praying for you."

"But sometimes I saw you on the footpath twice during the same parade!" the bandleader interjected.

"Yes, you probably did," Moy agreed, smiling. "If I could take a short-cut through side streets to see you more than once, I did so. On those days you were prayed for twice, or as many times as I happened to see you!"

The new convert had been struck dumb. He just sat staring across at this woman whom he had mistaken for an ardent loyalist when she had actually been standing by the roadside praying for him as he marched past proudly beating his big drum!

"And that's not all," Moy went on to finish her story. There was, she felt, just one final brush stroke need to complete the picture. "When I arrived back home at the farm after every parade I knelt down on the red tiled floor in the kitchen and asked God to intervene in your life."

Sammy felt the tears welling up in his eyes.

"Thank you," he said simply. He was totally lost for any other appropriate words.

Now he was beginning to understand why Peggy had not been surprised to learn of his salvation.

It was becoming clear that totally unknown to him, she, along with Mary and Moy and possibly many more had been praying that in some miraculous manner God would call Sammy to Himself.

And He had graciously answered their prayers.

Chapter Twenty Six

WHAT GOD HAS JOINED TOGETHER

When he arrived home from work on Wednesday 12 th March Sammy said to his wife over dinner, "I'm going up to the manse this evening to ask Rev. Courtney if he could arrange to dedicate our new band uniforms at a Sunday evening service sometime, Libby. Would you like to come with me?"

"Yes, I probably would, Samuel. It would take me out for an hour or so," Libby replied, in as matter-of-fact a tone as she could manage.

She had been secretly hoping for an opportunity to meet the minister somehow, for she had a burden on her mind. Although he didn't know it, her husband's conversion had made an indelible impression upon her. Her Samuel had become a completely reformed character, and she by then had begun to crave the peace and joy that could only be found in Christ, too. She had never been able to summon up the courage to tell him that, however.

On arriving at the manse, Sammy noticed that his wife remained unusually quiet. During the period he spent discussing the possible dates for and order of a uniform dedication service with the minister, she appeared uneasy. He thought that she looked very like somebody who had something important to say but was unsure just how or when to say it.

Still, though, Sammy didn't know what it was that was troubling her.

From the night of his conversion he had been praying constantly and earnestly that God would save Libby also, but he didn't realize that she was already concerned about her own salvation.

Rev. Courtney, with singular spiritual insight, noticed her edginess.

"Is there anything wrong, Libby?" he enquired gently, as the couple were standing in the hallway, preparing to leave. "Do you want to talk to me about anything?"

"Yes. I wouldn't mind a chat with you some day to tell you the truth," Libby confessed. "Call in to see me at the house when you have a minute."

"Don't worry, I will be down tomorrow morning," the perceptive minister promised.

As he set out for work next morning Sammy Graham was overwhelmed by an odd sense of occasion. He was sure that something, which would be certain to have a profound effect on the rest of his life, was going to happen that day.

Thus he was unusually subdued as he drove to his work in Lisburn.

Jim Lyons, his passenger, noticed it.

"You're very quiet this morning, Sammy," he remarked after an abnormally long silence.

"Yes, I suppose I am, Jim," the driver replied. "I'm thinking."

That was only partially true. Sammy was thinking. But he was also silently praying that God would guide Robert Courtney when he went to see Libby, and that she would give her life to the Saviour. He had prayed most of the way through his many wakeful periods during the night, and he was now thinking and praying his way to work.

It seemed a long time until tea break that morning but when it came around at ten-thirty, Sammy made a beeline for the single telephone in the site hut.

What frustration!

He had been painting and praying all morning until tea-break time when he could phone Libby. And what should confront him but one man standing roaring into the receiver about a load of cement which should have been delivered the previous day and a foreman waiting patiently with a site plan in his hand. He was planning, he said, to ring up the architect to discuss a snag they had come across when marking out the footings for a house.

At that moment in time Sammy couldn't have cared less about cement, snags or footings.

All he wanted to do was talk to Libby about commitment, salvation or faith.

He plunged out of the site hut and called to Jim Lyons. "Coming with me, Jim? I have to find a phone box somewhere!"

They drove around searching and eventually found a public telephone on the Ballymacash Road. This phone wasn't in a box but sitting up on a pole with a perspex shield over it.

"This must be the very latest in public phones," Sammy quipped as he jumped out of the rejuvenated P.O. van which Jim and he had bought to start their business.

When he had called home and Libby answered, Sammy's first question was, "Did the Rev. Courtney come round to see you this morning?"

"Yes, he did," his wife replied. "In fact he is just away about ten minutes."

After a short pause and a long intake of breath Libby went on, "I invited Christ into my life this morning, Samuel."

"I know! I know!" her excited husband replied at once.

Libby was astonished.

"How did you know?" she asked, completely flummoxed. "It only happened little more than an hour ago!"

"I knew because I was sure that God was going to do something marvellous in our lives today!" Sammy enthused. "It's great Libby! It's fantastic! And a mighty answer to prayer!"

There was no reply.

Libby had dissolved into soundless tears of joy.

"Are you still there, love?" her husband enquired, tenderly.

"Yes, I'm here all right, Samuel," she sobbed.

Soon Sammy was in tears too.

Then his money began to run out.

He reached over into the van and called across to Jim, "Have you any ten pees?"

Jim reached him out one.

It was soon finished, without Sammy having said one single word into the receiver.

Then he called in again, "Another one!"

It seemed to buy very little time either.

So Sammy leaned into the van and said urgently, "Quick Jim! Another one!"

"Hi Sammy, this is all my fag money I'm forking out to let you stand there and cry on the telephone!" Jim protested, and after he had parted with his fourth ten pence piece the commandeered coin supply dried up.

As he started the van to return to the job, Sammy attempted to explain his peculiar phone call.

"Libby has got saved," he told his workmate, struggling valiantly to control his emotions. He could be sure that Jim knew what he meant for he had been brought up in a Christian home, and Sammy had often spoken to him about spiritual matters.

Before beginning to paint again Sammy closed himself off in an empty room in the empty house he was painting and kneeling on the bare boards in the middle of the floor, with his elbows on two paint tins, he poured out his heart in thanksgiving to God.

"Thank You, Lord, for saving Libby," he began. "Thank You for answering all my prayers and the prayers of all the other believers who have been praying for her. Help us now to go on together with Your help and in Your love. Amen."

Sammy worked out the remainder of that day with a light heart and when he arrived home Libby and he hugged each other with sheer delight.

The new Christian showed her husband a list of verses Rev. Courtney had recommended that she should read, and when the boys had gone to bed later that evening they looked them up together.

John chapter three verse sixteen. John chapter five verse twenty-four. John chapter six verse thirty-seven. Romans chapter ten verse nine...

As they sat, with open Bibles in hand, on either side of the fire, tears began to spill down Sammy's cheeks once more.

"Now we belong to each other twice, Libby," he whispered, his cracking voice coming across as a croak. "We were joined together on our wedding day and now we are joined together in Christ. And what God has joined together no man can pull apart!"

Chapter Twenty Seven

COMMITTED TO THE WIND

It gave Sammy an inexpressible sense of fulfilment to have Libby with him at church every Sunday from that day forward. They were so together, united in love, in faith, in hope.

One Sunday morning in early summer an announcement, which immediately caught Sammy's attention and aroused his interest, was made at the end of the service.

'The Dick Saunders Way to Life team is coming to conduct a campaign in Dromara, starting next Sunday, and any able bodied men who are free are invited to go over there tomorrow and help erect the tent', was the gist of the message.

In the middle of the afternoon Sammy said, "You know, Libby, I think I should go over to Dromara tomorrow morning and give those men a hand to put up that tent."

"And what about your work?" was his wife's instant concern.

"I will phone Jim and tell him I am taking the day off," he told her. "It wouldn't do me any harm to give a day to God, and it shouldn't take any more than a day to put up a tent."

Sammy, though, was mistaken. For tents come in all sizes, and he had imagined the tent to be put up as being one of the type he remembered seeing in fenced-off corners of farmers' fields during the summer. That variety had two poles sticking out of the top of it, one at each end, and a closely cropped sawdust-covered path from the five-barred gate to the flap-type door.

When he arrived then, on Monday morning, Sammy was surprised at the size of the plot of land being marked off to accommodate the tent and the horde of men who had turned up to pitch it. At least forty men had assembled in the field, all ready for work, and in early afternoon the tent arrived, stacked high on a forty-foot trailer!

He hadn't been on the site long that Monday until Sammy realized two things.

The first was that if he was going to be of any use to this project he was going to have to give a week, and not just a day to God. The other was the soul-stirring discovery there were far more sincere Christian men out there in the community, all willing to devote their time and talents to the work of the Lord with the sole aim of seeing souls won for the Saviour, than he had ever imagined existed!

The week of work in Dromara proved to be a memorable experience for the new Christian. As he hammered in posts, dug holes, and helped lay out paths, Sammy counted himself privileged to be able to do so in the company of so many other believers. It was wonderful to witness men from different trades, and from a wide variety of evangelical church backgrounds, all striving together with a will, united in one goal for the Gospel.

Meal times, too, were something special that week.

Women from different church groups took turns to cater for the gang of workmen, some providing lunches, and others an evening meal every day. Sammy was impressed to see big strong men, built like tanks, slip off their caps and sit with heads bowed while one of their number thanked God for the food. Then after every meal and before they began work again they would all pray together for God's blessing upon the coming mission.

The other men didn't seem to consider this strange, nor did they find it particularly thrilling. It was simply what they did. They thanked God, prayed to God, and went on working for God, all without a lot of fuss.

To Sammy, though, it was all so refreshing and inspiring.

On Wednesday evening before they left the site, Ted, one of the men who had travelled with the tent, and was supervising operations, made what sounded to Sammy a rather peculiar statement when he was outlining the plan of work for the next day.

"Tomorrow, men," he declared to the group of helpers just before they returned to their cars to head for home, "we will be committing the tent to the wind."

What the foreman actually meant, the eager workman discovered on making a few enquiries, was that they were planning to haul up the canvas.

Committing the tent to the wind proved to be a fascinating, if occasionally frightening, experience.

There was a strong breeze that Thursday morning, so to prevent the canvas from blowing away before it could be secured some of the volunteers had to lie on it at the edges to pin it down. Then, as it was gradually pulled up the men were thrown upwards as the canvas was raised and the wind was allowed to enter beneath it. Sammy and a few others were catapulted into the air by the billowing canvas and landed with a heavy thud on the ground.

"Somebody's going to be killed here, before we get her up!" one man near Sammy exclaimed breathlessly, gathering himself up off the grass.

"Well, I'm all right!" Sammy called back, in the excitement and simplicity of his newly found faith. "I'm going to heaven!"

The foreman had said that they were going to commit the tent to the wind, and as he made that declaration Sammy experienced an uncanny sense of being committed to the wind of the will of God. He would be content to drift along in the divine draught, wherever it took him, or whatever it meant for him, for he felt so complete, so satisfied, in Christ.

The tent was eventually erected and it looked impressive, with its five huge poles protruding at the corners, pulling the canvas into the shape of a blue and white crown.

When it came Friday afternoon, and most of the work was finished, all the men who had laboured together in such harmony to erect the tent stood together in it, and prayed one after another that God would draw many souls to Himself in the coming two week campaign.

That earnest prayer meeting stimulated Sammy's spiritual enthusiasm. Working alongside so many genuine Christians for a week had done more for Sammy Graham's spiritual development than a month of teaching meetings could ever have done, and the patent sincerity of that final prayer time left him feeling that he never wanted to leave the tent. He felt that it belonged to him, or he belonged to it, somehow. All he wanted to do now was play some active role, however small, in the mission itself.

The campaign coordinators recognised the importance of involving such a capable and enthusiastic young Christian in the work, and they gave him a job.

Sammy was placed in charge of the heating and lighting in the tent. This was a practical task, which he was only too proud to be asked to perform, and to which he attended with great diligence.

For him one of the most exhilarating moments of every evening was the switching on of the lights in the massive tent. It was his job to peer through a slit at the back of the huge canvas cathedral, and when the pianist struck a chord with great gusto, Sammy ran both hands down a bank of switches with corresponding gusto, and the entire tent blazed into light.

On Monday morning, when he had returned to the more mundane pursuit of painting to make a living, Sammy, fired up with enthusiasm for the mission, and concerned for the spiritual condition of his friend, said, to Jim Lyons "Will you come over to Dromara with me to see the big tent some night, Jim?"

"What would I want to go and see a tent for, Sammy? Sure I have seen loads of tents in my lifetime," his workmate hedged.

"You probably have, Jim," Sammy conceded, undeterred, "but I would be prepared to say that you have never seen one like this. It is certainly the biggest tent *I* have ever seen!"

Thinking that he had perhaps majored too much on the properties of the tent, Sammy went on to elaborate by adding, "And the singing is marvellous and Dick Saunders is a great preacher!"

After some persuasion Jim agreed to go along with his painting partner on the Wednesday night. Sammy was delighted and told Jim that he would pick him up in good time for he had to be at the tent early since he had an important job to do.

Sammy then spent the next two days in fervent prayer for his friend.

On the first night that Jim went with him to the tent, Sammy showed him to a seat and then returned to his action station behind the partition at the back.

As the meeting progressed, and particularly as the preacher presented a simple Gospel message, Sammy peered though his slit and watched Jim to try and gauge his reactions. He was unable to come to any conclusion, but his friend appeared to be listening intently.

Sammy was pleased also, that Jim consented to go along with him, 'to the tent', two nights of the second and final week, but disappointed that when it came time to lower the tent to the ground, Jim hadn't become a Christian, despite much earnest prayer.

The seed of the gospel had been sown, however, and when the Way to Life Crusade was long past, the seed yielded a harvest.

In early September there was a knock on the door in Lisburn Street one Tuesday evening and when Sammy went to open it he found Jim Lyons standing outside.

"Come on in," Sammy invited and Jim stepped into the hall.

"I have something to tell you boy," he began without any preamble. "I'm just on my way in from a meeting out in Magheraknock. I got saved out there tonight!"

Sammy was overjoyed.

"Praise God!" he exclaimed. "Another prayer answered! Another soul saved!"

And another partnership had been set up.

The two men, who had worked together so often, had that evening become brothers in the Lord!

Chapter Twenty Eight

EIGHTEEN MEN ON A DOUBLE-DECKER BUS

For some years after his conversion Sammy continued to rejoice in his faith, and increase in his fervour for the work of the Lord. He had become actively and profitably involved in the Youth club and Boy's Brigade in his church, and yet he still longed to be even more useful to God in the spread of the Christian gospel and the encouragement of Christian people.

His big opportunity came in the spring of 1991 when he was invited to join a work party travelling to Russia to help refurbish a church in St. Petersburg. The aim of the organisers was to assemble a team of tradesmen who could spend a month in the summer working on a dilapidated building to help make it a more fitting base for an expanding church.

Sammy felt honoured yet humbled to be afforded such a chance to use his practical skills for his Lord, and accepted the invitation to travel with the team with a mixture of enthusiasm and apprehension.

He spent the following three months in preparation for the trip and was amazed at how God provided for his needs.

On a number of occasions kind wholesalers who supplied him with many of his painting requirements, but who were not, as far as Sammy knew, Christians, asked him, "Where are you going for your holidays this summer, Sammy?"

"You probably won't believe it but I am going to Russia!" the contracting customer would reply.

"Russia! What on earth is taking you to Russia?" was the sort of retort which usually followed Sammy's declaration of his proposed summer destination.

"Well it's a kind of a working holiday," Sammy would proceed to explain. "I'm going out to Russia as part of a team to help renovate an old church building in the city of St. Petersburg."

"That's a great idea!" some suppliers would reply, obviously impressed with the plan. "Can we help?"

"And how do you think you could help?" Sammy would go on to enquire.

"We could contribute materials to save you having to buy them," a number volunteered.

And they kept their promises, too!

Before Sammy was ready to leave he had been given one hundred and fifty gallons of paint, brushes, rollers and a host of other essentials of painting equipment.

The administrator of an abattoir in a local town even offered to donate a cow and two pigs to help feed the workers and the members of the Russian church.

"How do you think I could manage to transport a cow and two pigs to Russia?" Sammy enquired incredulously. There could be no doubting the man's sincerity but his suggestion was somewhat out of the question, Sammy reckoned.

"Don't worry!" the manager, sensing his listener's disbelief, went on to clarify the situation. "We will kill them and prepare them for you!"

And so it went on, until early July when Sammy met the other men who were to accompany him, and by then he was surrounded by a vast array of the tools and trappings of his trade. It was interesting to discover that what had happened to him had also happened to the plumbers and the plasterers, the electricians and the bricklayers as well.

They had all found people so big-hearted and open-handed. Everybody who heard about the project wanted to give whatever assistance they possibly could.

There was one huge logistical problem to be overcome, however.

How did one transport eighteen tradesmen with their bags of tools and many and varied essential items of equipment from Northern Ireland to Russia?

This problem was overcome through the generosity of the management of the Stagecoach Bus Company for when they heard of the men who needed transport to St. Petersburg, they made a double-decker bus available to the team. This bus even came complete with Christian driver, Jock.

On Tuesday, 2 nd July 1991, Sammy and seventeen other men set our on their big adventure for God. A few of them had never been on a boat before and yet they were setting out, fired up with enthusiasm, and with not a little faith, for Russia, to spend a month working for God.

They sailed from Larne and were met on the quay in Stranraer by Jock and his brightly coloured double-decker bus. When they had stored what they had brought with them in all available space on the bus they had a short time of prayer and then set off. They were on their way!

That journey proved to be a wonderful time of bonding for the team. They talked together, prayed together, and were afforded many opportunities to witness to their faith.

A double-decker bus full of men who seemed to have a tremendous sense of unity of purpose amongst them aroused much curiosity, especially on the sea-crossings.

People would ask some of the men, "Where are you going on your bus?" Or, "What kind of a summer holiday is this? Is it some sort of a working men's bus tour?"

This allowed Sammy and the others to tell of the purpose of their trip to Russia, to work on the church building, and to explain the motivation behind it, which was their love for the Lord and His people.

On the crossing from Harwich to Europe Sammy was invited to have lunch with a pair of Canadian businessmen who showed a keen interest in the project and then asked Sammy how he had become involved. This gave the painter from Ballynahinch an opportunity to tell them how he had come to know Christ as Saviour and how he was now eager to serve the Lord in some practical way, to help repay in some hopelessly inadequate measure, the blessings he now enjoyed in Christ Jesus.

The men were mesmerised at the story, confessing to never having 'heard the like of that before'.

When Sammy was leaving them he promised to pray that they also might find the peace, joy and satisfaction in salvation, that he had found.

They journeyed for days, eating where they could, stopping for a few hours sleep at nights, and praying frequently.

Eventually they reached the Russian border.

This was to be the big test.

Would they be allowed into the country with all the load of stuff they had brought with them?

The prospective church restorers, who had come so far, had reached their final hurdle. They sat in the bus at the border and prayed one after another that God would help them make the crossing easily.

And God answered their prayers.

After a few questions and a superficial search of the bus the customs officials allowed them through

They were in Russia! Reckoning that it was wrong to ask God for His help without thanking Him for supplying it, the eighteen men on the double-decker bus were joined by Jock the driver when they stopped two miles inside the country and held an impromptu praise and prayer service.

They had much for which they felt bound to thank God, but there was so much about which they still needed to pray, for they hadn't as yet reached their destination.

When they were halfway between the border crossing and St. Petersburg the weary travellers stopped the bus, on a piece of flat land beside the rough road for a meal and a rest.

Having had something to eat, the men on the team were just

considering packing up to resume their journey when two cars drew up. Within seconds four men and two attractive young women, dressed only in bikinis, had spilled out of them and approached the startled bus party.

They were, they thought, in a quiet rural location, and nobody could possibly know who they were or where they were. Yet these people had found them on their meal stop and were soon offering the men an unlimited supply of vodka, and the services of the young women, all at 'greatly reduced prices'!

It took the Christian work party some time by a series of gesticulations and some vigorous shaking of the head, to persuade the men who had called with their special offers, that they weren't really interested in their proffered goods or services. They did persuade them to accept some Gospel booklets in Russian, and eventually the four men and two women piled back into the cars and left.

Sammy, Jock, and the other seventeen had survived their first encounter with the Russian Mafia!

It was late on Saturday night, almost six days after they had set out, when the bus with its cargo of exhausted travellers arrived in St. Petersburg.

Some of the men were to sleep in the bus for the duration of their stay in the Russian city, but Sammy and the remainder were to stop over in a hotel.

Conditions in the hotel were basic by British standards but Sammy and his friends were so tired they reckoned they could sleep anywhere.

Meeting in a bedroom a few of them praised God for His continued protection and care, and as they parted to retire each to his own quarters they remarked to one another with a genuine sense of satisfaction, accompanied by a huge sigh of relief, "Well at least we have made it! We're here!"

And with the next day being Sunday they were set to have their first look at the church building they had come to restore, and their first opportunity to meet at least some of its congregation.

What would that be like? Sammy wondered to himself before drifting off to sleep.

Chapter Twenty Nine

IT MUST BE LIFTED HIGHER

Church next morning proved to be a memorable experience, though not perhaps for the reasons Sammy had imagined.

Since the main sanctuary of the building had to be vacated because of its disrepair awaiting the attentions of the work party as soon as possible, the morning service was conducted in a large downstairs room.

The service was due to begin at eleven o'clock and when Sammy and his friends arrived ten minutes before the time they found the place packed to capacity. Whether it was because there were no other seats available, or whether it was to give the visitors maximum exposure, Sammy wasn't quite sure, but what he did know was that he found it embarrassing to be marched, with the others, and their interpreter, Nadia, right up to the very front row.

When the worship began, the warmth of the wholehearted singing and the sincerity of the prayers impressed Sammy immediately. Although he didn't understand a word of it he was quite convinced that these people were in vital touch with God and they knew how to praise Him and to pray to Him. There could be no doubt that their faith was vitally important to them.

With the preliminaries over the speaker read the text for the day from the Scriptures and after he had finished reading and had begun to speak Sammy found himself confronted with a simple dilemma. Having closed his Bible, he had nowhere to set it down. Being right in the very front row he had no chairs in front under which to place it.

He held it in his hand for almost half an hour by which time it had begun to become sticky with perspiration from the palms of his hands, and since the preacher showed no signs whatsoever of being anywhere near finished, Sammy set it on the floor and slid it gently in below his seat.

The address was being delivered in Russian, and the interpreter couldn't risk speaking too loudly in case she should upset others in the congregation, so Sammy found it difficult to follow proceedings. With the combined effect of the stuffy heat of the crowded room on a hot July day, his tiredness from the marathon bus journey, and the fact that the address was much longer than any he had ever heard back at home, he also found it very difficult to remain awake. Despite valiant efforts to prevent it, he began to slip off into the realms of sleep in snatches.

As soon as the speaker had finished, however, Sammy was shaken back to consciousness for good. He was unceremoniously jolted back to reality!

Someone from behind was tapping him fiercely on the right shoulder, with pointed fingers piercing mercilessly into his skin through his light summer shirt.

Sammy jerked around with a start to be met with the fixed and obviously upset, if not even angry, gaze of a small, elderly woman. This lady had a black shawl pulled tightly around her head and the wrinkled, wizened face, which it framed in stark relief, bore its own testimony to a lifetime of poverty and privation. And she was holding Sammy's Bible in her hand.

In the instant their eyes met, the little lady launched into a flood of Russian, her body trembling, and her voice rising almost to a shriek at the end of occasional sentences.

The only pause in the tirade came when she stopped to draw breath, and she didn't dare waste those seconds either. In her breathing spaces she tapped, with a gentleness totally inconsistent with her apparently aggressive attitude, the Bible she held in her hand.

Sammy didn't know any Russian but he didn't need to know the spoken language to understand the body language of the woman who was addressing him. Although he had no idea why at that particular moment, he very soon realized that he was being severely reprimanded.

The lady was certainly deeply displeased about something.

Mortified at having become the focus of attention on his first morning in the church he had come to help, Sammy turned to the interpreter and whispered, "What is the lady saying?"

Nadia leant across and replied, her face blushed bright red, "She says that you should never leave the Word of God on the floor. It should be lifted higher!"

When she was satisfied that the offending visitor had been given the message in his own language, the little lady handed Sammy back his Bible, with an air of respect, and resumed her seat.

Sammy held his Bible in his lap until the end of the service.

He had learnt his lesson.

The lady behind hadn't finished with him yet, however, or perhaps it was he who wasn't finished with her!

At the end of the service, which had lasted for almost four hours, Sammy stood up in preparation to leave. He was glad of the opportunity to move his aching limbs once more and banish the pins and needles from his legs for good. There was very little noise as the congregation filed out in dignified reverence, and Sammy was taking it all in, savouring the amazingly awesome atmosphere which had been generated in that simple downstairs room.

Suddenly he became aware of the little old lady who had been sitting directly behind him.

She had her back to him but Sammy was tall enough to see over her shoulder.

The lady who had remonstrated with him for placing his Bible on the floor had spread a square of deep blue silk cloth out on the chair in front of her. Then, setting her tiny Bible in the middle of the square she began to fold it up carefully in the square of silk. When this operation was completed she proceeded to open the small ragged cloth bag she was carrying and slip her silk-wrapped parcel slowly into it.

Sammy Graham was pierced to the heart.

He had come to Russia, as part of a team, imagining that he and his friends, with their practical skills, guaranteed financial backup, and superior spiritual understanding, would be able to help the poor, deprived Russian people in a multitude of different ways.

Now he knew that he had been sadly mistaken.

As the thin little lady moved out slowly in front of him, Sammy stared intently at the back of the black shawl, still pulled tightly over her white hair.

He had been profoundly challenged by the respect of that simple person for the Holy Scriptures, which he took so readily for granted.

Was it possible that instead of coming to Russia to help people, God had sent him there to be helped?

It certainly appeared a distinct possibility.

The lady had said that the Bible shouldn't be left on the floor.

It should be lifted higher.

He had been transported on to a higher plane already.

And he still hadn't been a full day in St. Petersburg.

Chapter Thirty

MAMA VERA

Sammy worked diligently with all the others during that busy four-week stay in St. Petersburg, and by the end of the month the main sanctuary of the church was well on the way to completion.

It was a rewarding experience.

Working together in close cooperation with other dedicated believers proved a spiritual impetus to Sammy in very much the same way as the Christian teamwork essential to the erection of The Way To Life tent had done. He learnt more about the love of God in action on the ground, and the importance of a united goal in Christian service in those four weeks than he could ever have done sitting through a year of meetings.

Although the work party from Northern Ireland had been enlisted to perform the specialist tasks and provide the funds and materials, the members of the church laboured tirelessly in support of the team. During those long, sometimes hot, but usually hard, working days, Sammy met a number of the local Christians on a one-to-one basis and the more he came to know them, the more he came to love them.

One person whose godly grace impressed itself upon the painting adviser on the restoration team, was Vera Zakharovna, a lady who Sammy reckoned to be in her mid-to-late sixties. This woman, referred to affectionately by most as simply 'Mama Vera', seemed unusually highly respected by all for some reason. It soon became clear that her advice was often sought on a wide variety of both practical and spiritual matters. Sammy gathered from observation, and in conversation with the interpreters, as the days passed, that Mama Vera's home served as a haven for many in the church in times of difficulty. She dispensed food and clothing to poor families where needed, and when she had the resources available.

At the end of their stay, when the party was packing up to set off for home, happy that their task had been successfully completed, but sad at the prospect of parting from newly made friends, a major complication arose.

The bus had broken down, and as spare parts were unavailable it had to be left behind.

This meant that the eighteen workmen, plus Jock the driver, who had all reached St. Petersburg in the brightly coloured bus were faced with a daunting prospect. They were left with no option but to make an arduous and tiresome journey by sea and land across many national borders before arriving in Larne harbour five days later.

Libby met her husband when he came off the boat and he was so utterly exhausted that he declared emphatically, as they were driving back to Ballynahinach, "That's me finished, Libby. You won't have to put up with me running away again. Don't get me wrong, I enjoyed every minute of my time in Russia but all that travelling is a killer. Whoever likes can go again, but I'm quite sure I'll never be back!"

Or so he said!

For months, too, that was how he felt.

Then slowly, gradually, his attitude began to change.

He couldn't seem to get the believers in that church in Russia, out of his mind.

When he stood up to pray in a prayer meeting he thought of their passionate prayers.

When he sang some of the hymns, which he had only recognised in Russia by their tunes, he thought of their hearty singing.

And when a preacher, who had spoken for half-an-hour or maybe forty minutes, said almost apologetically, 'I must close now for the time is up,' he thought of some of the speakers in Russia who thought nothing of preaching for an hour and a half or perhaps two hours! And that without feeling any need to apologise for it either!

Sammy's impulsive declaration on his return from his summer term in Russia had disregarded one all-important consideration. And that was the purpose of God for his life.

For God had permitted St. Petersburg, and some of its saintly people, to become, in the month he had stayed there and been with them, an integral part of his being, without him ever realising it.

In early 1993 a number of men told Sammy that they were planning to go out to the Russian city to do evangelistic work, distributing Gospel literature, and asked him if he would like to accompany them.

It didn't take Sammy long to make up his mind!

His proclamation of almost two years previously was rendered null and void, when he stated his intention to join the team.

Before he set out, Libby who had heard so much about the church and its members from her enthusiastic husband, and was ever eager to encourage him in the work of the Lord, said, "I will pack you a suitcase full of good clothes, for that woman you call 'Mama Vera' to use."

Libby's care and consideration left Sammy with the responsibility of contacting Vera at some stage in his stay to deliver the clothes to be distributed to those in most need.

He met 'Mama Vera' at church on his first Sunday back in St. Petersburg and arranged through Nadia to go and visit her in her home on a night during the week. Nadia very kindly agreed to be there also to act as interpreter.

In the course of that evening Sammy began to appreciate why so many of the people in the church community held Mama Vera in such high esteem. When she felt comfortable and confident in Sammy's presence, and following a little gentle persuasion from Nadia and some of the others present, Vera Zakharovna told Sammy Graham a most remarkable story.

Vera had been brought up in a Christian home in St. Petersburg, which was then known as Leningrad, and as a child had trusted in Christ as her Saviour.

When she was just thirteen years old, on 1 st September 1941 German troops, as part of their offensive on the Eastern Front, began a siege of her city. Hitler had ordered that Leningrad was to be taken by 'a bloodless occupation' and so his troops surrounded the city, severing all vital food supplies and communications, confident of forcing the citizens to surrender.

He has grossly underestimated the resolve of the Russian army and the residents of Leningrad, however. Vera described how she, although still little more than a child, helped all the able-bodied population of the city, men, women and children, to build antitank fortifications around the city in support of the 200,000 Red Army soldiers stationed there.

It turned out to be a long and horrendous siege.

With winter approaching and food supplies cut to a mere trickle, people began to die. Funerals became an everyday occurrence.

Conditions became terrible and people became desperate.

When Hitler realized that the people were not going to be easily broken he ordered his troops to begin attacking the city with heavy gunfire.

650,000 people died from starvation or were killed by German bombardment in 1942.

And still the city refused to surrender.

The blockade ended when Russian troops broke through the German lines and relieved the city in January 1944. During the nine hundred days of the siege almost one million people had lost their lives.

When she had finished her graphic description of some of the horrific happenings of those days, Vera said softly, "But we survived. We kept praying to God and trusting in Him, and I believe that He brought us through."

Before he left Vera's home later that night Sammy promised to come back and see her every time he retuned to St. Petersburg. He felt drawn to this modest woman who had been through so much, sustained by a simple Christian faith.

He kept his promise, and on every subsequent visit to the city he called with Vera.

Then Sammy received a wonderful invitation. The church members were planning a special service to celebrate the life of Mama Vera to mark her seventieth birthday. Would he come, and if possible bring Libby? Their presence was to be a surprise for Mama Vera and the highlight of the event.

Although Libby had never been to Russia before she felt that this was an invitation which she couldn't possibly refuse, and so she and Sammy attended the thanksgiving service in St. Petersburg.

What a moving experience that proved to be.

Men lined up to testify how Mama Vera had been either instrumental in pointing them to faith in Christ, or influential in guiding them in their Christian lives.

There was much joy when Sammy and Libby appeared on the platform with that gracious, godly lady.

Libby enjoyed her first visit to St. Petersburg and it was thrilling to meet all the people that she had heard Sammy mention so often. It was helpful to be able to put faces to names. It would allow her to pray more intelligently in the future.

Mama Vera had made her two specially invited guests promise that they would call to spend an evening with her before they left for home, and on the night before the were due to return to Northern Ireland they went to her apartment.

The evening was spent in pleasant conversation, for they felt so close to each other, as though they were tied together by some strong, invisible bond.

Just as they were rising to go Vera said through her interpreter, "I have something I would like to give you, Sammy."

"And what's that, Vera?" her friend enquired, totally unaware of what was coming.

"It's this," she replied in a whisper, reaching deep into the pocket of her brown dress.

She held a small box out towards Sammy, and when she opened it a gold medal glinted in the dim light of the room.

"And what's that, Vera?" Sammy said for the second time,

stunned. He didn't realize that he had asked the same question twice, in his embarrassment.

"It's my Leningrad medal," Vera went on softly. "All those who survived the siege were given a medal to mark the event. I look upon you as a true son, and I want you to have this."

She then closed the box and attempted to place it in Sammy's hand.

Her 'true son' was shocked and closing his fist, placed his hand behind his back.

"No Vera, I can't take that!" he protested. "That is too precious to you!"

"It is not really precious, Sammy. But you are precious, and the Lord is precious, and I want you to take it for His sake. Every time you look at it you can remember us here in Russia. And please pray for us," Vera replied gently, but firmly.

Sammy unclenched his fist, stretched out his hand, and Vera placed her medal in it.

By that time tears had welled up in the eyes of everybody except Vera. Everyone was touched by her selfless generosity.

"Thank you, Vera. Thank you," Sammy tried to reply, struggling to find appropriate words to express his deep gratitude. "You are giving me your medal but God has something even more precious reserved in heaven for you. It is a crown, a crown of righteousness which the Bible says the Lord the righteous judge will give to faithful Christian people in a coming day."

It was then Vera's turn to be touched.

Tears began to stream down her cheeks too.

She smiled broadly, and nodded enthusiastically.

She was looking forward to that day.

And had been for nearly seventy years.

Chapter Thirty One

SHE'S BLIND!

An increasing desire to see at least a few of the constantly moving mass of people who thronged the streets of St. Petersburg every day reached with the good news of the Gospel of Jesus Christ, compelled Sammy to return to Russia, year after year.

In the early summer of 1997 he and Gordon Campbell went out to distribute Christian literature on the streets. They found people eager to accept the attractive coloured booklets depicting the life of Christ, when they were offered to them. Many Russians love to read, but since books were often expensive, and wages low, the opportunity to procure some interesting reading material free of charge, seemed too good to miss!

Some grateful recipients, fearing a catch, even stopped to enquire why people should be so kind as to give them an appealing and professionally produced booklet absolutely free.

What was the snag? Did they need to read some small print?

Their curiosity afforded Sammy and Gordon the opportunity, through their interpreter, Galena, to witness to the wonders of God's love and His provision of free salvation to all who trust in Jesus.

The work was encouraging and many profitable contacts were made but the two men felt like stones skimming across a lake. They were only touching the surface of the problem with an occasional contact here and there. They hadn't broken the surface of a total incomprehension of Christianity, and they certainly weren't creating any waves, or even ripples, to wash back onto the shore and make a difference. The bulk of the population of St. Petersburg remained unaffected by their daily vigil for God on the streets.

"What we need," Sammy said to his friend as they trudged back to their lodgings at the close of their third day there, "is a contact in a school or college or some place like that where we can reach a number of children or young people at once."

"I think you are right, Sammy," Gordon agreed. "We should make it a matter of prayer."

It was all they could do.

So for the remaining days of their planned stay, every morning before they set out, and every night before retiring to bed, they prayed earnestly that somehow God in His infinite power and wisdom, would open the way for them to present His Word and hence His truth, in a school or college in St. Petersburg.

On the face of it, and to the casual observer, this would have seemed like a crazy request.

How could two complete strangers, with no background in education, ever hope to make contact with a school in a large city in a foreign country?

Despite their faith and fervent prayers, it looked as though their vision of an invitation to visit a school was not going to be fulfilled.

How could it be, anyway?

Surely it was nothing more than a pipe dream? Mere pie in the sky

They began to give up hope when they reached the final morning of their trip to Russia without contact having been made with any educational establishment.

Perhaps God had just decided to whisper a gentle, "No", to His zealous servants' ridiculous request.

Having packed up to go home, the only appointment that Sammy and Gordon had to keep on their last day was a lunchtime meeting with Galena, their interpreter, and Danny her eight-year old son, in a city centre restaurant.

Galena had been so diligent in all her work for the two Gospel literature distributors that they were anxious to show her some small token of appreciation in return.

Their interpreter had been thrilled to receive their invitation. A meal in one of the large downtown eating-houses was a luxury she couldn't normally afford.

And Danny, she had assured them, would be delighted.

When lunchtime came and they met up at the restaurant Sammy was surprised to see Danny all dressed up in his best suit and tie. He thought of some of the children in the cafes back home with the knees out of their jeans, jazzy T-shirts and baseball caps on back to front.

What a contrast!

This was Danny's big day.

When he stepped inside the door his face was a picture. His eyes almost popped out in disbelief as they scanned around the monster posters advertising triple-decker burgers, double Cokes, and huge mouth-watering ice creams.

Galena had to order for them all, and when it came to Danny's choice he found it difficult to decide. Both he and his mum were afraid of asking for too much and causing their hosts unnecessary expense.

Sammy spoke across to her and said, "Order him up the biggest burger he can eat."

With all imagined restrictions abolished Galena did just that. She picked out what she thought Danny would like from the huge overhead menus and ordered it.

What a treat for Danny and his proud mum.

They really did relish every moment and every course of that meal, but almost as soon as it was over Galena became very business-like once more and announced, "Now it is time for Danny to go to school."

Sammy was taken aback.

"It's after two o'clock in the afternoon, Galena!" he responded involuntarily. "What does Danny have to go to school at this time of the day for?"

"School for Danny begins at three o'clock," the interpreter felt she ought to explain. "There are so many children attend his school that half of them go from early morning until two o'clock and the remainder, Danny's half, begin at three and continue on into the evening."

"Oh, I see," Sammy replied, his instinctive curiosity satisfied. There never had been all that big a demand on the local Primary School back in Ballynahinch.

Then he paused for a moment to figure out his programme for the afternoon.

"We have to take a taxi to the airport," he mused. "So we will take you with us, call at our lodgings and collect our cases, leave you and Danny off at the school, and then make for the airport in time for our flight."

It all sounded so easy and so sensible.

When the taxi drew up at the school door, however, Danny stepped out onto the footpath and began to repeat one word in Russian.

"What is he saying?" Sammy asked his mum.

"He is saying 'Come. Come'. He is inviting you into his school to meet his teachers and the Direktor. You would call her a headmistress, I think," was how Galena interpreted her son's urgent invitation.

"O.K. We will come," Sammy accepted at once. Then conscious of their tight schedule he added, "But we won't have long to stay or we will miss our plane. Tell the driver to wait for us."

As they walked in through the main doors of that large school Sammy felt so unworthy. Gordon and he had been beseeching God all week to open the doors of a school to them, and when they had all but given up, an eight year-old boy was leading them into a massive school, where almost two thousand pupils were taught every day.

Danny led them straight to the Direktor's office and after Galena had spoken to a secretary, they were admitted into the presence of the lady in charge of the school.

Sammy stepped forward to shake hands with the Direktor as she rose from her seat but his outstretched hand evoked no response. He dropped his hand down to his side again just as Galena whispered into his ear, "She's blind."

They had a short conversation together, with Galena who acted as interpreter explaining that the two men had come to Russia to give out booklets telling about Jesus.

Before their interview finished the Direktor said, "You are welcome in my school. You can visit any classroom you wish and speak to any teacher you wish. Do you have enough booklets for all our pupils?"

Sammy thanked her for her warm welcome but had to confess that he didn't have enough booklets for every pupil, but promised to return as soon as possible with one for every child in the school.

When they stepped out into the corridor Sammy said to Gordon, "You go to that end of the corridor and pray, and I will go to this end. Let us pray that God will guide us into making the best use of this opportunity He has granted us of reaching every child in this school with His Word."

As Galena was leaving them out to the taxi, ten minutes later, Sammy had something on his mind.

"Tell us about the headmistress. Has she been blind from birth?" he wanted to know.

"No. She hasn't," Galena informed him. "She has cataract."

"Cataract!" Sammy replied, astonished. "Sure a simple operation would fix that!"

"I know," Galena went on, quietly. "But she probably can't afford it. There is no National Health scheme here, and operations can be expensive."

"Oh, I understand now," said Sammy, his mind slipping into overdrive.

After a frantic drive to the airport the two prospective passengers were just in time to board their flight home.

As the plane roared down the runway before take-off Sammy sat with his eyes closed.

"Are you O.K.?" his friend enquired.

"Don't worry about me, I was just praying there," came the reply.

"And what were you praying about, or should I not ask?" Gordon pursued the subject.

"Guess!" Sammy countered with an impish grin.

"Let me think," his companion made a great show of deep deliberation before responding to the challenge.

"You were thanking God for letting us into Danny's school and you were praying that He would help us to somehow pay for a cataract operation for the headmistress," he volunteered at length.

"Dead right, Gordon! How did you know? You have hit it spot on!" Sammy was forced to confess.

"After all," he went on to reflect, "how can we possibly go back to that kind lady and tell her that God loves her, if we don't do anything to try and help her?"

Chapter Thirty Two

SIGHT AND LIGHT RESTORED

The plight of Danny's school Direktor gave Sammy and his friends a focus for prayer for the remainder of that year.

Requesting prayer from Libby and his many concerned Christian friends was only the start of Sammy's campaign to have something done about the school headmistress. Although his intention had been to use prayer as the sole launching pad for his crusade he began to be showered with donations from genuinely caring people keen to help in a practical way.

A major obstacle arose to his best-laid plans when he began to attempt to negotiate with hospitals in St. Petersburg to try and make definite arrangements. Sammy needed to find out if he could locate a hospital in the city willing to perform the operation, how much it would cost, and when the blind lady herself would be free to have the sight-restoring surgery performed.

Communication, from a distance, by a not always reliable telephone network, and only when one could be assured of the services of a capable interpreter who could be trusted to deal with all calls in the strictest of confidence, proved something of a nightmare.

Sammy often became frustrated.

It was maddening to be so anxious to do something which he considered to be in line with the will of God in the circumstances, and for his life, and yet find himself thwarted at every turn when attempting to make progress with it.

After many futile phone calls and pursuing a number of dead end trails Sammy had a return call, which cleared up the entire situation, once and for all, from Russia one day. The message was one of good news but Sammy found part of it puzzling.

The headmistress with the cataract had been for successful surgery and was now rejoicing in being able to see again. That was the baffling bit. How had she been able to afford the operation? her would-be benefactor was anxious to know. Where had the funds come from?

For weeks Sammy endeavoured to find out who had sponsored the surgery for he wanted to offer to share in the expense, but his efforts proved fruitless. The most he could learn was that 'an anonymous donor had come forward'.

The other item of news was more exciting.

The school's Direktor wanted to know when the kind men were coming back with the books for the children.

What a challenge!

And what an answer to Sammy and Gordon's seemingly impracticable prayers of seven or eight months before!

An invitation to deliver Gospel literature to almost two thousand children represented a unique window of opportunity to someone eager to place a Bible in the hand of every child in that school.

God had furnished him with the funds, too, for the gifts donated to bring sight to a headmistress could easily and justifiably be redirected to bring the light of life to the pupils in her care.

Now the agonising days of uncertainty and indecision were over.

Sammy had a goal to aim for and much to keep him busy. Russian Bibles had to be purchased and arrangements made to have them delivered to the school.

When he was actively engaged in preparing for the biggest distribution operation of his life up until that time, an interesting contact was made. It occurred too, not when Sammy Graham, Christian literature collector was buying Bibles or packing boxes, but when Sammy Graham, painting contractor, was working along with his men, decorating a church.

One afternoon the minister of Ballygowan Free Presbyterian Church, Rev. Derek Erwin, called in to check on the progress of the painting, and to try and establish in his own mind 'when these boys were going to be finished'.

In the course of casual conversation he asked the question, "When are you planning to go back to Russia, Sammy?"

"God willing I hope to be going back out in a month or two," Sammy replied, giving no indication as to the purpose of his visit.

"That's good," the minister replied, obviously pleased at the proximity of Sammy's proposed visit, for he had a specific reason for his earlier enquiry. " I was just wondering if you would have any use for two hundred leather bound Russian Bibles when you go out? We used to give them to sailors down at the docks and since we no longer do that we have a surplus of lovely Russian Bibles."

Sammy could barely believe it!

God had intervened to solve another one of his niggling problems. Bibles for the children hadn't proved too difficult to procure but what was he going to give the teachers? He had been trying to think of something special to give them, and now he had his answer.

"I certainly could use two hundred leather bound Russian Bibles!" Sammy exclaimed, and then went on to explain how.

And when he entered the church next morning, there they were, left out for him. Two hundred beautiful Bibles in a box on a table at the front.

Gordon, who had been so involved in the first visit to Danny's school, accompanied his friend back to St. Petersburg when the pieces were in place for the all-important Scripture drop.

Their initial task on arriving at their destination was to locate the premises of a Russian colporteur who, after a series of telephone calls had arranged for them to procure large quantities of, 'My First

Bible', for younger children and other Bibles for the more senior pupils. When looking at the stock of literature in the colporteur's store Sammy spotted, and bought, fifteen copies of a large illustrated Bible. These, he reckoned, would be marvellous for the school library.

Sammy and Gordon began the day designated for the visit to the school with a time of prayer for guidance before Vladimir picked them up in his small minibus. Vladimir was a local Christian who had volunteered to transport the Bibles from where they had been purchased to the school.

It was an indescribable thrill for Sammy and his friend to witness the eager courtesy with which every person in the school received his or her copy of the Word of God.

They began with Nadia, the Direktor, presenting her with a leather bound copy, and she arranged for them to visit each classroom and present a copy of the Scriptures to every pupil and a leather-bound Bible to every teacher.

All the children loved their new Bibles but the younger pupils were particularly delighted to be given their 'First Bibles' for they were written in Russian with an English translation. Some of them observed happily that their 'new books' would help them with their English lessons. Sammy even suspected that he saw some of the school staff eyeing them enviously!

The two men and their much wider back-up team, all of whom had invested so much prayer and effort into placing the Bibles in the school didn't care why they were read, as long as they were read. And judging by the enthusiasm with which they had been received, they had every confidence that they would be.

That, too, was merely the morning session! The entire process had to be repeated to another equally eager school full of pupils and staff in the afternoon.

It was as they were about to leave finally, at the end of the afternoon session, that Gordon and Sammy presented the grateful headmistress with the fifteen library copies.

She was most appreciative and assured the two benefactors that they would be placed in the library that day, and made available to every pupil and teacher in the building.

As Sammy and Gordon returned to their lodgings in the evening it was with a genuine sense of achievement, and a deep sense of gratitude to God.

The sight of a blind headmistress had been restored and the light of the Word of God had been placed in the hand of every pupil in her school.

They quoted to each other, and to God in the course of their grateful praise and earnest prayer more than once, the words of Psalm one hundred and nineteen, verse one hundred and five.

'Your word is a lamp unto my feet, and a light unto my path.'

Its rays, they knew, could do much to illuminate the lives of all they shone upon, not only in Russia, but also all over the world.

Chapter Thirty Three

WHO WAS NUMBER FIVE?

Later that same summer Sammy was back in Russia.

He and some others had helped fund a Christian camp for young people and he was keen to be there as a leader, giving whatever assistance he could.

As he moved around the camp during the week Sammy was impressed by two things. The first was the attention that the campers paid to the Scriptures as they were read and explained, and the second was the dedication of the younger leaders to the Lord and in His service. They threw themselves unstintingly into the work. Nothing seemed too difficult for them provided it would serve to advance the cause of the Gospel amongst the boys and girls at camp.

Two of the younger lady leaders showed a particular aptitude for dealing with the children placed in their care. They were Yula and her friend Yana.

Yula was a radiant Christian who had just completed her training as a midwife. It seemed that wherever she moved around the camp she had a number of children trailing in her wake. Her personality attracted them like a magnet.

Sammy made a point towards the end of the week of encouraging Yula, Yana, and a number of the promising young men to develop their potential for youth and children's work. He was convinced that God could use talented, dedicated local believers like these to be a most effective witness for Him in their bustling home city.

At the end of the camp Sammy went off to Moscow for a few days but when he arrived back in St. Petersburg he began calling all the leaders from his hotel to check that they had arrived home safely.

When he rang Yula she assured him that she had indeed arrived home safely and had returned to work on Monday. She then went on to enquire, "Where are you ringing from, Sammy?"

"I'm in a hotel here in St. Petersburg," he replied.

"Why don't you come round to our flat and meet my mother and my sisters," Yula invited. "They have heard so much about you, I know they would love to meet you."

"And where would I ever find where you live?" Sammy enquired, fearful of becoming lost in a busy city.

"Take a taxi to…" and then Yula gave Sammy the name of a street or road which he couldn't even make the slightest attempt to pronounce.

"I couldn't even say the name of that place, never mind find it," Sammy joked. "Put your receiver down and I will phone you back in a minute or two!"

Sammy then ran downstairs and said to a receptionist in the lobby, "Could you possibly phone that number for me?" and pushed Yula's number across the desk on a scrap of paper.

Always anxious to please, the receptionist did as requested, and when Yula answered it the receptionist handed the receiver back to her, as she thought, flustered, guest.

"Hello there, Yula. Hold the line a minute," he instructed. "I'm going to bring a taxi driver in here and you can give him those directions."

"Great idea!" Yula laughed. "Who would have thought of it!"

When the taxi-driver had been given the address of the flat in which Yula lived with her family he set off through the streets which teemed with traffic of all sorts. Sammy sat relaxed in the back of his cab not having a clue where he was going, confident that he would somehow, sooner or later, arrive at his destination.

It took almost twenty minutes before the taxi-driver pulled up at the end of a street where Yula was waiting. The light rain which had flattened her hair down onto her head was causing her face to shine in what remained of the evening light.

"Oh Sammy, I am so glad to see you again!" she exclaimed enthusiastically, after her guest had paid his driver. "Come, come and meet my family!"

With that she set off briskly, Sammy stepping along beside her.

Having crossed two streets they came to an apartment block, and Yula approached a ground floor flat.

When she had knocked the door a woman in her forties came to open it. Sammy recognised her at once.

"This is my mother," Yula said by way of introduction. "Her name is Valya."

"I think I have met you before," Sammy ventured to suggest. "Were you not helping to work in the church when I came to Russia first in 1991?"

"Yes, I probably was," Valya replied, quietly.

Sammy knew she was. He had often remarked to some of the others how hard the women had worked on that project.

"Any one of these women could mix and carry more cement than any two men back home," he remembered quipping to a workmate near him one day.

And Valya had been one of those women who had laboured to the bricklayers, mixing cement and carrying it in buckets into the church.

"Come and meet my two sisters," Yula urged, and Sammy followed her into the living room to be introduced to Helen who was seventeen and Dacha who was just six.

Although he couldn't speak their language, and Yula and Helen were the only two of the family reasonably fluent in English, Sammy felt immediately at home among these people. The genuine warmth of their welcome was unmistakeable and he was soon to discover that an uncanny sense of peace and contentment seemed to pervade their home.

They sat around and talked for some time and then Valya prepared a simple meal for them all.

When the meal was over Yula said something to her younger sister, and then interpreted for their visitor.

"I have just asked Helen to sing for you," she said.

Helen smiled coyly, then stood up.

And when she began to sing Sammy Graham was mesmerised. He had heard many solos in churches in his Christian career, and many vocalists with dance-bands for years before that, but never in his life had he heard anything like this.

He wished that the world would stand still so that Helen's singing wouldn't have to stop. She had such a clear ringing voice.

As in all church services in Russia, so again in that home that summer evening, Sammy had to recognize the piece by the tune, but he had no difficulty doing that.

It was 'How Great Thou Art.'

Every time Helen returned to the chorus it seemed to be with more vigour, and renewed sincerity, so much so that Sammy just felt like shouting out, "Amen Lord! Amen! How Great Thou Art!"

After she had sung a second piece Helen sat down and took a sip from her glass.

"That was brilliant, Helen! Absolutely brilliant!" Sammy enthused, and he meant every word of it.

Helen flushed bright red with a satisfied embarrassment, and mother anxious to spare her blushes focussed the spotlight away from her, and onto her little sister.

"Dacha will say some verses for us," she announced.

With that little Dacha, who was just six-and-a half and had serious health problems, stood up and began to repeat something in Russian.

Yula leaned across to Sammy and whispered, "Psalm twenty-three."

Then when she had finished and sat down, she too glowed with pleasure when Sammy was equally wholehearted with his praise.

"That was brilliant, Dacha! Absolutely brilliant!" he said.

They talked on for almost half-an-hour before Sammy declared reluctantly that he would have to return to his hotel.

"Yula will call a taxi for you," Valya, mother and controller of the house told him. "And while we are waiting for it we will read the Scriptures together."

Reaching over to a shelf beside her she picked up the well-used Bible that Sammy had noticed soon after he had entered the room, and opening it she began to read.

"John chapter fourteen," Yula whispered across, smiling, soon after coming in from the telephone in the hall.

When the honk of a horn indicated the arrival of his taxi, Sammy found it difficult to drag himself out of that flat and away from those people.

He somehow felt that although he had only met four people, five people lived there. There was a holy but happy, relaxed but reverent atmosphere about the modest ground floor flat.

Later in the evening, lying in bed staring up at the dim ceiling, Sammy thought of a Bible story he had been reading before leaving home.

It was about two disciples, who had asked Jesus out of curiosity, "Master, where do you live?"

As he remembered it, Jesus had replied to her enquiry with the invitation, "Come and see."

Earlier that evening Sammy had been invited to come and see where Yula lived, and to meet her family, and in responding to her invitation he had discovered the answer to the disciples' question.

Jesus lived with the Deneatcheva family.

Chapter Thirty Four

A LESSON LEARNT IN RUSSIA

Having made contact with so many committed Christians, and having seen so many Bibles distributed not only in Danny's school, but also in the huge prison in St. Petersburg, Sammy felt compelled to take a further step of faith.

It was insufficient just to fly into Russia, work hard for a few weeks, and then disappear again until the following year.

Something more permanent needed to be set up, a work which could carry on in his absence.

Since Valya and her family, Mama Vera and many others had to travel some distance to their existing church, it would be wonderful, he reckoned if a small Christian witness could be established in their area. This would serve a dual purpose. It would provide the local Christians with a more convenient place of worship, and it could also be the beginning of a Gospel outreach in another district of the large city.

The most obvious problem with this concept, though, was that Sammy felt strongly such a group needed a dedicated leader or pastor with a burning desire to serve God, and when he first considered the possibility of commencing another outreach, he didn't know of anybody.

He decided to make his vision a matter of prayer and he asked a number of interested Christians, both in Northern Ireland and in Russia to do the same.

A few months later he had a call from Mama Vera. She had encouraging news.

"I think I ought to tell you about a man I have just met recently," she said earnestly. She had the air of someone who had given the matter much thought before lifting the receiver. This, to her, was a serious affair. The person she was about to suggest could eventually end up being her pastor. "Some friends have introduced me to a young man who is attending the Bible Seminary here in St. Petersburg. All who know him consider him to be a man of God."

Sammy was delighted.

Was this God's answer to his prayer?

"That sounds interesting, Vera," he replied, eagerly. "What's his name? Tell me more!"

"He is called Sergei Vicktorovich and he is married and has a teenage daughter. I have spoken to Valya and Yula and some others about him and we honestly believe he would be an ideal person to lay the foundations of a work for God in this part of the city."

Valya gave Sammy a telephone number and in January 1999 he made contact with Sergei and arranged to travel out and meet him in the spring.

On reaching St. Petersburg Sammy lost no time in arranging a meeting with Sergei and discovered all that Vera had said about him to be true. Here was a man who had a deep love for God and during their time together it became evident that his sole aim seemed to be to please Him in all he did.

"What do you want most in life, Sergei?" Sammy asked at one point in their conversation.

"There are two things which are most important to me," the possible new pastor replied, simply. "I want more than anything else to glorify God in my life, and to see other people, men, women, boys and girls, led to trust the Saviour."

"You are just the sort of person I have been praying that God would lead me to," Sammy confessed, having heard that statement of intent.

Then he went on to probe a little further.

"Did you ever envisage having a church of your own, Sergei, where you could preach the Gospel and pastor a congregation?" he enquired.

"I have never thought of it as being a prospect for me, at least in the near future," the committed Christian worker admitted readily. "But if I was sure that it was God's will, and if He would open up the way, I would certainly have to consider it."

They spent many hours together that day, and on subsequent days, before Sammy had to leave, and on each of those occasions they prayed together for wisdom, seeking a sign from God.

If it was His will for them to commence a church fellowship in that particular sector of the city, He would make a suitable building available.

He was barely two weeks back home before Sammy received an unusually exuberant e-mail from Sergei. God had answered their prayers, he felt, for he had just been offered the use of a building which could easily be converted into a church.

There then followed a series of urgent calls to Russia, dealing with both practical and spiritual concerns.

What alterations, if any, did the building require? How should they go about informing the local people of their existence, and inviting them along? What should be the form of service?

On a Sunday, three weeks later, Sergei held his first Sunday morning service with nine of a congregation. Valya was there with her three girls, Mama Vera, Sergei's wife Helen, their daughter Kysusha, and two others. God was there too, and it was the unmistakeable sense of His presence which made that first meeting so memorable.

Although not present at their initial meeting Sammy was thrilled when he heard of it.

It wasn't long either until he had arranged another trip out to Russia to acquaint himself with the most pressing needs of the work.

He hadn't been many hours with the happy group of believers who were so pleased to have their own church fellowship near their home until he was told of their most immediate requirement.

"What we really need now is for our group to be registered with the authorities as a church, with me as its pastor," Sergei explained.

"Well then, what's the problem?" Sammy wanted to know, unaware of all the legal requirements. "Let's go and register it."

Sergei looked solemn.

"Unfortunately it's not just quite that simple," he went on. "For me to be registered I need to own my own home, and I'm afraid that is impossible. I am now living in a rented apartment and I will probably do so for the rest of my life."

"It may sound impossible to you, Sergei," Sammy responded to the young pastor's very practical pessimism. "But remember there is nothing impossible with God."

Sammy was a step ahead of Sergei, for he had already learnt that lesson through his former experiences in Russia.

Before leaving him to return home yet again he gave Sergei specific instructions. "You go and look for a suitable property to buy in this district," he told him, "and leave the rest to God. I am going home to pray fervently about this."

For days after he arrived home Sammy began to have his doubts. Had he been too outspoken to say that God would do the rest? Where was the money going to come from to buy an apartment in St. Petersburg, even if Sergei did manage to find a suitable one for sale?

Despite the doubts Sammy still tried to convince himself that God would intervene and show His mighty hand in the situation, somehow.

He was right.

Inside two weeks Sergei phoned to say that he had located the ideal apartment, and told Sammy the asking price.

Now came the challenge.

How was he ever going to raise such an amount of money?

But he felt he had to. And he still believed there was nothing impossible with God.

During that period of the summer Yula was making her second visit to Northern Ireland to spend a holiday with Sammy and

Libby. She loved it, and her presence with her two friends at the services in Ballynahinch Congregational Church helped focus the minds of many of the members on Russia, without Sammy ever having to mention it. She was a walking, talking, shining, smiling visual aid.

After the midweek meeting Sammy, Libby and Yula were invited to Sammy's mother's home for supper with another couple. In the course of conversation the only other man in the company enquired, "How's the work going in Russia, Sammy? Is there anything particular you need?"

"Yes, in fact there is," Sammy felt compelled to share with this patently interested person, and he went on to outline the Sergei situation. He spoke of his talent, his commitment, the manner in which they had been afforded the use of a building for a church, and Sergei's need of a home of his own so that the church could be registered.

"That is amazing," the listener replied, as soon as he had heard the story. "I believe God has been telling me for days to speak to you about Russia. I would like to help share in the purchase of an apartment for the pastor. Hold on there a minute."

He then proceeded to pull a chequebook from his pocket and write.

And when he had slipped the cheque he had written across to Sammy it was his turn to be astounded.

The amount he had donated was exactly half of what Sergei's apartment was expected to cost!

That was only the start.

Ballynahich Congregational Church donated the offering from their Harvest Thanksgiving Service to the work in Russia, and Sammy and two other young men from the church, David English and John Miskelly, did a one hundred mile sponsored walk to raise funds.

Six weeks later he set off on his third trip of the year to St. Petersburg with the total amount required to purchase an apartment for Sergei in his possession.

It was eleven o'clock on a Friday night when Sammy arrived at Sergei's rented flat.

On hearing that Sammy had brought with him all the necessary funds to buy him his own apartment Sergei said at once, "We will give the solicitor a ring and arrange to meet him in the morning."

"You can't ring a solicitor now!" was his tired friend's instant reaction. "It's eleven o'clock at night! And tomorrow's Saturday, anyway! He will be off!"

"Of course I can," Sergei replied, smiling. "Our solicitors work long hours, and six days a week. We will see him in the morning."

They did too.

By early afternoon that Saturday Sergei had been given the keys to his new apartment. On their way back to it from the solicitor's Sammy and Sergei called to collect Helen and Kysusha.

The expressions of delight bordering on disbelief on the faces of that little family as they moved about the apartment as though in a dream, will live with Sammy Graham for the rest of this life.

And their prayers, as they later moved systematically from room to room, dedicating each one in turn to God made an indelible impact upon him.

Each of them spontaneously and wholeheartedly thanked God for His ability to do far and away beyond anything they had ever asked or thought.

They told God humbly, and with tears of overflowing joy, that they had just learnt another lesson. It was the lesson He had chosen to teach their friend Sammy since he had started coming to their country.

There is nothing impossible with Him.

Chapter Thirty Five

THE LIGHT OF THE WORLD

As Sergei and his family settled into the new home which they constantly recognised as being but a part of God's bountiful provision for their lives they felt a responsibility towards their new neighbours. They wanted to tell them of the love of God for them, but deemed it important to first demonstrate that love in a practical way to those around them. So Helen and Sergei began to invite their neighbours into their home, to get to know them and to take the opportunity to tell them about Jesus.

Gradually entertaining more and more of the people of the district in their apartment helped forge a link between the Viktorovich family and their neighbours. Then when Sergei asked them if they would like to come along and hear him speak in the small fellowship which had been called the Church of Christ's Resurrection, many came.

A wave of spiritual gratitude swept over Sammy when he and Libby visited the church in August 2001. Having opened its doors for the first time just over a year before, with a pastor and a congregation of nine, the church had, by the date of their visit, over seventy Christian members. Another great cause for rejoicing was the fact that there were at least one hundred and fifty people present that summer Sunday morning.

The hearts of the visitors were touched when they heard the story of Kirill. When he had been making his announcements Sergei had implored the congregation, "Please continue to pray for Kirill, for we believe that our God, with whom nothing is impossible, can do marvellous things for him."

Sammy smiled quietly at the announcement, but it aroused his curiosity as well. Obviously Sergei was continuing to prove the power of God in his life and ministry, but who was Kirill? And why did God need to do marvellous things for him?

After the service he made a few enquiries, and met Kirill, whom he discovered to be a nine-month old baby boy who had been born blind. His mother had come to know the Lord Jesus Christ as her Saviour just a few months earlier and had joined the church. Now Sergei and his concerned congregation had made the lovely little blind boy's condition a matter of earnest and consistent prayer. He had been having regular medical attention and his mum had been told that if he would ever be able to see, and it was 'a big if', then major surgery would be required.

Sammy and Libby felt so sorry for the young mother and her baby that they also pledged themselves to pray that God, who had created Kirill's eyes, would heal them completely and he would be granted the blessing of physical sight.

When they arrived home Sammy asked his friends in Ballynahinch Congregational Church to pray for the little blind baby boy, too.

In late September there came a most encouraging telephone call from Sergei.

The pastor sounded extremely pleased. "Praise God, Sammy. Praise God," he began, his words tumbling over each other as he spoke in a stream to the interpreter who had the task of translating his excited babble for the man at the other end of the line. "Kirill's mum has just called around to let us know that she has taken him to the hospital for a regular check-up and the doctors think an operation may not now be necessary. The condition of his eyes has begun to improve and they are convinced that, though it may take some time, his sight will come back naturally and he will have at least partial vision!"

His call did two things for Sammy Graham. Firstly it made him all the more determined to pray for baby Kirill that his sight might be restored not just partially, but completely. And it did something else as well.

It caused Sammy to look back on his life.

He thought of his days in the darkness, painting the town red, planning all sorts of mischief, running and hiding from God in every dark sinful corner he could find.

Then there was the night in his bedroom when the light of the truth of salvation through faith in Jesus Christ burst in upon his soul and lit up his life for God.

Since then he had been privileged, both at home and in Russia to see that light spread through the presentation of copies of the Scriptures and the establishment of a church for the preaching of the Gospel.

What a thrill!

The light of the love and grace of God was still shining abroad, allowing its beams to penetrate into dark and hopeless situations.

He had discovered, though, that in a spiritual sense he was still only partially sighted himself.

For every day he seemed to be unearthing new treasures of truth in the Bible and experiencing some further evidence of the power and presence of God in his life. These successive, step-by-step revelations had proved precious to him.

He felt a lump rise in his throat as he contemplated a day still to come when he would no longer be partially sighted, seeing something fresh every day, but he would see his Saviour in all His radiant beauty, face to face in heaven.

That he thought will be real vision. That will be, glory for me...

His reverie was interrupted by the telephone ringing again.

It was the secretary of the Christian Union in a local College.

"Sammy, we had a committee meeting a few days ago and I was asked to contact you on a couple of matters," a young woman's voice explained. "We would like to know when could you possibly come and tell your life-story at one of our Tuesday evening meetings, and we would also like you to tell us how we can become involved, even in some small way, in the work in Russia? We would like to do something, anything, to help."

That brought Sammy down to earth with a bump.

He hadn't reached heaven yet.

There was still much to do.

He would continue to tell as many as he could about the Light of the World for as long as he was left in the world.

For the Light of the World is Jesus.